D0765215

BUILDING A LOVE THAT LASTS

BUILDING A LOVE THAT LASTS

Outstanding articles on marriage from the Ensign

Deseret Book

Salt Lake City, Utah

©1985 Deseret Book Company
All rights reserved
Printed in the United States of America

No part of this book may be reproduced in any form or by any means without permission in writing from the publisher, Deseret Book Company, P.O. Box 30178, Salt Lake City, Utah 84130

First printing September 1985
Second printing March 1986

Library of Congress Cataloging-in-Publication Data
Main entry under title:

Building a love that lasts.

1. Marriage—Religious aspects—Mormon Church.
2. Marriage—Religious aspects—Church of Jesus Christ of Latter-day Saints. 3. Mormon Church—Doctrines.
4. Church of Jesus Christ of Latter-day Saints—Doctrines. I. Ensign (Salt Lake City, Utah)
BX8641.B83 1985 248.4′8933204 85-16011
ISBN 0-87747-852-X

Table of Contents

I. *A Daily Commitment*

II. *Showing Love and Affection*

III. *Chastity in Marriage*

IV. *Sharing Feelings*

V. *Resolving Differences*

VI. *Managing Money*

VII. *Loving an Inactive or Nonmember Spouse*

A DAILY COMMITMENT

Love That Lasts

Although time and circumstances may alter a couple's expectations, vision and commitment can keep love constant.

By Kathy England

Whenever my husband and I need a good laugh, we pull out a small stash of folded hotel stationery tucked within our family Bible. Neatly scrawled there are the goals we outlined for ourselves in front of a bright fire in a small skiing cottage on our honeymoon. Looking at those idealistic goals, I remember both of us, hugging in front of the fire, determined to make our marriage a very happy, successful partnership. And that it is—despite the fact that a number of the goals listed on those carefully saved papers have long since been replaced by reality—and two stubborn, loving individuals working together.

Our goals covered everything from finances to exercise, including a decision never to spend over twenty dollars for an unbudgeted item without consulting each other.

But only two months after our marriage, I came home from school one afternoon to discover my entrepreneuring husband, Lan, sitting on our one piece of furniture, a tiny couch, leafing through an airplane parts manual. "You'll never believe what we bought today!" he announced in unrestrained glee.

"What did *we* buy today?" I asked, a sudden foreboding warning me to sit down.

"Last night in the classifieds, I read about this fantastic deal out at the Bountiful Airport. A local insurance company is selling a Grumann two-seater for a lady in Phoenix."

"A Grumann two-seater?" I asked weakly.

"Yes. A beautiful little plane. Lists for $15,000 in good condition. We got it for $2,000."

"Two thousand!" I was beginning to feel quite faint.

"Can you believe it! We got it at that price because the lady ran out of gas and had to land it in a field. Coming down she went between some trees and peeled the wings back." Lan's enthusiasm didn't abate, but my shock only deepened after we drove to the airport and climbed into the cockpit of our small red plane without wings.

It was on the way home, when the numbness began to wear off, that I thought to remind him of our list of goals. "Oh, I remembered," he admitted, with all the charm of a little boy who has just been to see Santa Claus, "but I knew you'd understand on a deal like this. I had to act fast or it would be gone."

We owned the plane for only four weeks. Without doing much repair work, Lan sold it for a profit.

Since then I have learned to appreciate the business sense and creativity of my husband, but learning to trust his decisions has meant giving up one original honeymoon goal. And that is not the only goal that has been changed or replaced. Identifying and eliminating unrealistic expectations has trimmed our list into a workable blueprint for a fulfilling marriage.

But that sorting-out process is not an easy one! Curious, romantic beings that we are, we build many expectations before marriage. From watching other marriages, reading books on compatibility, listening to "experts," we begin to sketch in our minds a picture of the perfect marriage. Yet our picture may be slightly, even dramatically, different from our companion's. And when those different expectations start surfacing—right after the honeymoon—it takes both vision and commitment to sort out a realistic blueprint both partners can live by.

The necessary vision of who your partner really is—the ability to see beyond an irritating moment into the eyes and heart of the person you love—makes the sorting-out process easier; it becomes a strengthening, bonding experience instead of a weakening drag on your relationship. It requires accepting the other and choosing to interpret his or her actions and intentions with love, not doubt.

At the temple marriage ceremony of our niece, Cindi, the wise priesthood leader who presided taught the principle of vision with a few simple questions. Cindi knelt, all in white, radiant, shyly smiling across the altar at Steve, his smiling eyes also filled with sweetness and love. All of us tasted the joy of this beginning as we watched those smiles.

"Steve, look at Cindi," Brother Bay said. "Isn't she beautiful?" A wordless, powerful nod answered him. "Can you imagine her doing anything wrong right now?"

"No," he said softly.

Brother Bay turned. "Cindi, you look at Steve. Isn't he handsome?"

"Oh yes!" she smiled across the altar.

"Can you imagine him doing anything wrong today?"

"No," she said, smiling again.

Lan and I smiled too with an inward joy, remembering our many mistakes, yet savoring still our vision of each other.

"Never forget your feelings now, Cindi and Steve. Always look for the best, and you will find it."

Reflecting on Brother Bay's counsel, I could see how, one by one, our unrealistic expectations had been stripped away, revealing the practical, operating bones of our relationship. We had grown in love, compassion, and the ability to grow and be flexible. We had learned patience, trust, and loyalty.

But it is our vision of each other that makes it worth the time and pain such lessons have been bought with. This vision of each other helps us look beyond the momentary frustrations and trust in each other's true nature and potential, despite problems. But we must *choose* how to look at our companions, and the way we choose will determine our response.

For three months I had been diligently studying the May 1980 issue of the *Ensign* and all the sesquicentennial general conference talks. Our stake was sponsoring an *Ensign* competition as part of our sesquicentennial celebrations, and our bishop had recruited *me* to absorb the entire issue from cover to cover. As the evening for the competition loomed closer, I studied during every spare moment, nervous and filled with excitement, but very grateful for all I was learning.

Two hours before the game began, my husband received a call from his mother. "King's been hurt," he announced to me, worry streaking his eyes. "I've got to go."

"But, honey," I began.

"I'll try to be back," he yelled as he headed for the front door.

"But what about the children? I'm supposed to sit on the stage."

"I'll take them with me." And two minutes later, they were gone. Now, in case I seem unfeeling, it may help to know that King is a cat. Not just any cat, but a remarkable sixteen-year-old cat who had slept on the foot of Lan's bed for over ten years before he married me. Lan and King were old friends. But a cat is a cat, and a wife is a wife, I told myself, as I sat there seesawing between fuming and laughing.

Ten minutes before I had to leave, Lan called from the veterinarian's office. "They're going to operate. King's hip has been wrenched out of its socket."

I tried to keep the tears out of my voice. "How long do you think it will take?" I asked.

"I don't know. But good luck tonight, honey! I know you'll do really well!" We both hung up, and I started listing in my mind all the reasons to be upset. After all, tonight was my big night! I'd worked on this for months! Couldn't someone else sit in the waiting room?

But fortunately, I knelt to pray for some last-minute courage. And I received not only courage but patience, and another way to look at the situation. I realized how blessed I was to have a husband who was sensitive and caring about creation. And that quality of tenderness didn't end with animals. That same protectiveness and love was magnified as it extended to me and to our children. Besides, I knew he really loved me, and it was not like he was putting King first. I felt almost like chuckling at my initial perspective. Then I remembered that even the sparrows and the lilies of the field were loved and cared for by God.

Choices exist in every situation, and training ourselves to have vision is as simple as slowing our response-time long enough to say a prayer and consider alternate views. When Adam and Eve received the joyous news that through the Son's sacrifice they might earn the right to live with the Father again, they rejoiced in their new-found vision of life.

"And in that day Adam blessed God and was filled, and began to prophesy concerning all the families of the earth, saying: Blessed be the name of God, for because of my transgression *my eyes are opened,* and in this life I shall have joy, and again in the flesh I shall see God.

"And Eve, his wife, heard all these things and was glad, saying: Were it not for our transgression we never should have had seed, and never should have known good and evil, and the joy of our redemption, and the eternal life which God giveth unto all the obedient." (Moses 5:10-11; italics added.)

Truly, through their problems, Adam and Eve learned to see, to know the good from the evil. We inherit this gift of mortality, the ability to see, and the agency to choose for ourselves. How we use this vision can sometimes make an eternal difference in our lives.

But along with vision, one more quality is essential if love is to last. And that is commitment. Even with vision, the separating of unrealistic expectations from potential goals is painful. But if we are committed to the marriage, that determination gives us strength and helps us find creative ways to endure in our love.

I'll never forget a conversation I had one afternoon on the way home from work riding on a bus next to a pert, older woman. She had remarked that soon she would be celebrating her fortieth wedding anniversary with her husband.

"You know why many marriages fall apart nowadays?" she queried, her eyes snapping. "They don't have any glue! I'm not perfect, and neither is my husband, but we're happy. And you know why? Because we've had enough loyalty to each other to hang together through our problems, and each problem we've resolved has been like a drop of glue, holding us together. After forty years, there's a lot of glue," she winked at me, chuckling softly, "there's a lot of glue."

Determination to endure. Loyalty. Commitment. Of such is the glue that holds people together when they've lost their vision. Commitment is the shelter, the healing place, for bruised and weakened love. The importance of commitment was brought vividly home to me through the personal experience of a close friend.

"Shortly after our first wedding anniversary," she related, "deep and shattering depression engulfed my husband. Satan-fed fires of self-doubt consumed him, and he struggled with insecurity, losing the ability to love himself. In his misery he confessed, 'My mind tells me I love you, but I can't feel it. I just don't know how I feel anymore.'

"For two weeks, I hung on the edge of those words, not sleeping, not tasting life. But in my anguished prayers, the Lord held out a lifeline. He helped me understand that my husband couldn't love me until he could love himself again. With that insight, I found the strength to hope, to hang on. I held fast to my eternal sense of John's worth, to the son the Lord loved so dearly.

"When he lashed out at his wrong choices and himself, I quietly reaffirmed my faith in him. Repeated words of love and faith over two months finally broke through John's negative self-image. We emerged from the experience more strongly committed to each other. John freely admits that without the unwavering commitment and love he felt from me during those months, he doesn't know where he would be, where we would be."

The final refuge for all of us is the Savior's love. His atonement was the perfect expression of love and commitment. He marked the path we all must follow if we are to gain the commitment and vision necessary to endure to the end in love. "Love one another," he told us, "as I have loved you." (John 15:12.)

And there is the key. The Savior sees each of us as we are, knowing who we can become, but loving us as we are. He beholds us with perfect vision and welcomes us with love that is both patient and eternal. That kind of Christlike love, that kind of vision and commitment, gives us the room to sort through our false expectations and emerge with an ever-growing capacity to share the gifts of life eternally.

Kathy England, mother of three, is an in-service leader in the Salt Lake Park Stake Relief Society.

Individual Liberty, Commitment, and Marriage

The idea of irrevocably committing oneself to spouse and children seems out of fashion in these days of "liberation."

By Bruce C. Hafen

I once learned an important lesson about commitment. One of our children came home from school and announced that if he did not finish a certain project by the next day, he was going to be in deep trouble. His fourth grade class was completing a study unit on Indians, and he had the assignment to build a diorama on a cookie sheet, showing graphically the habitat of a certain Indian tribe. For several reasons, it really was critical that he successfully complete the assignment that night. When I came home from work, my wife, Marie, had already spread out on the kitchen counter most of the materials for the diorama. My son was stomping around the kitchen in great frustration, wanting to finish his project, but not wanting to start on it.

After supper, I assumed (since it was Monday) that we would be proceeding with our plans for family home evening. However, Marie said that she felt our fourth-grader had to finish the diorama then or never, and that she had made some decisions that would make it possible for him to finish. Not completely understanding, but taking her word for it, I herded the other children into the living room where we did a few things that passed for home evening.

Periodically, I heard outbursts from the kitchen as the

diorama builder insisted that he wouldn't do another thing. But not once did I hear from his mother the kind of response I think I would have given. At one point, I went in to her and insisted that if he couldn't be more considerate, we would forget the whole thing. But she gently encouraged me to let her proceed with her plan. That I did, amazed at her calm attitude.

Eight o'clock became nine and even later. I was just tucking the other children into bed when into the bedroom they came. Our fourth-grader, grinning proudly, was carrying his diorama like a birthday cake. It was obvious from looking at it that he had made every piece of it himself. As all the others gathered around, he pointed out to them each item: bark, wigwam, tree, and miniature animals. I glanced at my wife. She was smiling tranquilly.

Our boy placed his diorama on the bedroom counter and went over to his bed. Looking back at his mother, he grinned broadly. Then, though he wasn't usually demonstrative, he ran back to her, threw his arms around her waist, and gave her a boyish, awkward look of genuine appreciation. In that moment, they exchanged unspoken thoughts of much meaning. Then he raced back to his bed and we left the room.

Touched and amazed, I asked, "What on earth happened? How did you do it?" Marie replied that she had just made up her mind that nothing he could do could make her raise her voice or lose her patience. She had simply decided in advance that no matter what he said or did, she would keep encouraging him and helping him, even if it took all night. Then she made this significant observation: "I didn't know I had it in me."

She didn't know she had it in her. And she never would have known had she not made the commitment that leaving him, either literally or figuratively, was simply not an alternative. It would have been perfectly reasonable for her to throw up her hands after an hour of honest effort and send him out of the kitchen. But her commitment would not permit that. And so she discovered a reservoir of patience and endurance within herself that she didn't know was there. She and my son also discovered a higher dimension in their relationship—all because of her commitment.

Somehow, the idea of irrevocably committing oneself to

spouse and children seems out of fashion in these days of individual liberation. There is almost endless talk about personal liberty and self-fulfillment; it is in the air, everywhere. There are "rights movements" not only for minority groups and women, but also for children. However, the leaders of these movements—to leave their advocacy undiluted—seldom talk about the serious problems that could be created by a wholesale adoption of their goals. A line from one of the ballads of the student rights movement of the late 1960s reads, "We want our rights, and we don't care how."

This current obsession with individualism has already begun to affect attitudes toward marriage and family life. Strangely, the sacred idea of individual liberty—when carried to its extremes—also contains the seeds of selfishness, the enemy of marriage. Sensing these risky undercurrents, one modern writer has thoughtfully expressed concern about the tendency to blame marriage and family for what some consider their own lack of self-fulfillment:

"People say of marriage that it is boring, when what they mean is that it terrifies them: too many and too deep are its searing revelations. . . . They say of children that they are brats. . . , when what they mean is that the importance of parents with respect to the future of their children is now known with greater clarity . . . than ever before.

"No tame project, marriage. The raising of children . . . brings each of us breathtaking vistas of our own inadequacy. . . . [So,] we want desperately to blame [family life,] the institution which places our inadequacy in the brilliant glare of interrogation. . . .

"Being married and having children has impressed on my mind certain lessons, for whose learning I cannot help being grateful, though most of what I am forced to learn about myself is not pleasant.

"The quantity of sheer . . . selfishness in . . . my breast is a never-failing source of wonder. I do not want to be disturbed, challenged, troubled. Huge regions of myself belong only to me. . . . Seeing myself through the unblinking eyes of an intimate, intelligent other, an honest spouse, is humiliating beyond anticipation. Maintaining a familial steadiness whatever the state of my own emotions is a standard by which I stand daily condemned. A rational man, acting as I act? Trying to act fairly to children, each of whom is temperamentally different from myself and from each other, is far more baffling than anything Harvard prepared me for.

"My dignity as a human being depends perhaps more on what sort of husband and parent I am, than on any professional work I am called to do. My bonds to them hold me back from many sorts of opportunities. *And yet, these bonds are, I know, my liberation. They force me to be a different sort of human being, in a way in which I want and need to be forced.*" (Novak, "The Family Out of Favor," *Harper's*, Apr. 1976, p. 37; italics added.)

In other words, "I didn't know I had it in me."

The author of this passage senses at an introductory level what the gospel teaches in fully flowered form—marriage is one of the Lord's primary institutions for perfecting the individual. In the intimacy of the marital relationship, our true selves are exposed and tested enough to permit the discovery of capacities that are in fact great reservoirs of potential character growth. Testing, learning, and growing at this depth are simply not possible in less intimate, short-term relationships. It is not really that difficult to be polite to Church, business, and social associates. But only the truly compassionate are patient and unselfish with those who, over many years, share their possessions, their checkbooks, and their name. Thus, marriage has the power to develop Christlike character, if those who marry submit themselves to the schoolmaster.

Misunderstandings and differences of opinion are normal marriage; they are not a sign that a marriage is in trouble. The real issue is how a husband and wife respond to the natural stress and strain. Our *attitude* about what happens is far more important than what actually happens. The key element in those attitudes is commitment—a commitment to wait, to listen, to live with imperfection, to "nourish and cherish" as Paul wrote in his beautiful passage on marriage in Ephesians 5:28-29. This is a commitment never to leave, literally or figuratively, temporarily or permanently.

Thus, far more is at stake in typical marital differences than may be apparent on the surface, because when this kind of commitment wanes, the discovery process also wanes, and so does the process of personal growth. Not understanding the depth of the commitment made through the act of marriage and perhaps influenced by seductive talk about their "right to self-fulfillment," many in today's world who experience marital differences elect to leave the scene of the conflict by either literally or figuratively divorcing themselves from the person they view as the source of their frustrations.

Many of these in time will marry another person, only to find another set of conflicts and frustrations. Once again, they may leave the scene of conflict, somehow believing that they are entitled to live without the inconvenience of dealing with points of view different from their own. ("We want our rights, and we don't care how.") Thus, they may never experience what it is to understand a situation from the perspective of another person or to subordinate their own needs to those of others. As a result, they deprive themselves of the experiences necessary to permit the discovery of the meaning of love. They actually cheat themselves of the learning opportunities of mortality. On the other hand, those who are deeply committed put themselves in a position to make some remarkable discoveries about their spouses and about themselves. Significantly, these discoveries may have profound effects upon individual character development.

If we are not compassionate in marriage, we are probably not compassionate in any important sense. Therefore, we are not Christlike. But if our commitment in marriage is wholehearted, it will not matter what kind of difficulty arises or why it arises; leaving will not be an alternative. In time, through that commitment, our ability to see things from our partner's point of view and our capacity to control the intensity of our reactions will grow gradually, until we can be unselfish with not only our companion but with everyone else. That will be our real liberation.

When the Savior comes, those who will be able to live with him will be those who have learned, through experience, to live as he does. *Celestial* means "Christlike." Thus, those who have developed Christlike personal attributes will be celestial men and women, and the marriages of which they are a part will be celestial, eternal marriages—not merely in duration, but in quality and kind. But for those of the shallow commitment, the selfish heart, and the proud mind, it will not be possible to live with their partner or with the Savior in the eternities. They won't have learned how. Even the Lord cannot endow us with celestial personal attributes as if they were our "right." If that were possible, He would have done so long ago. Our "right" is the opportunity to develop our attributes by applying true principles in the environment of marriage.

In the conclusion of Charles Dickens' *Little Dorrit,* a new marriage is depicted as the beginning of a *descent* out of which the only important kind of *ascent* is possible:

"Then they went up the steps of the neighbouring Saint George's Church, and went up to the altar, where Daniel Doyce was waiting in his paternal character. And they were married, with the sun shining on them through the painted figure of Our Savior on the window. And they went . . . to sign the Marriage Register. . . .

"They all gave place when the signing was done, and Little Dorrit and her husband walked out of the church alone. They paused for a moment on the steps of the portico, looking at the fresh perspective of the street in the autumn morning sun's bright rays, and then *went down.*

"Went down into a modest life of usefulness and happiness. Went down to give a mother's care, in the fulness of time, to Fanny's neglected children no less than to their own, and to leave that lady going into Society for ever and a day. Went down to [be] a tender nurse and friend to [those in need]. . . . They went quietly down into the roaring streets, inseparable and blessed; and as they passed along in sunshine and in shade, the noisy and the eager, and the arrogant and forward and the vain, fretted, and chafed, and made their usual uproar."

Thus did Little Dorrit go "down into a modest life of usefulness and happiness." Those who view the quiet contemplation of the church house as the essence of the religious life might not understand how there could be great religious meaning in going "quietly down into the roaring streets, inseparable and blessed" into the "usual uproar" of common, everyday family life. But if there is no religious meaning in the ordinary uproar of family life, there is not much religious meaning to life at all. That is where heroism, sacrifice, virtue, and the power and blessings of the priesthood are most likely to be discovered and practiced.

Of course, to "go down" from our pedestals of pride and selfishness into such experiences is also to slip beneath the level of the visible, and the Lord's work done within the walls of our own homes will not be in full view of an outside audience. For that reason, the lessons learned, the service rendered, the attitudes shaped, the lives quietly changed by the fruits of a true commitment to marriage will never be widely known or understood by outside observers. The principles of love and commitment, and the silent satisfactions that flow from them, are private matters of the heart, known only to those who practice them. Yet, there are no more meaningful satisfactions, for in going down, we ultimately may go up, to the peace and the glory of celestial life.

Bruce C. Hafen, dean of the law school at Brigham Young University, serves as a Regional Representative for the Church.

The Formula That Saved Our Marriage

"For the next thirty days," he suggested, "let's think only of the other person's needs."

By Judith A. Long

"Are we going to make this marriage work, or not?" he asked. Seven months married, six months pregnant, I sat on the bed, tears streaming down my cheeks and spotting my nightgown. I couldn't give my husband an answer.

Jim, a nonmember, and a lieutenant junior grade aboard a U.S. destroyer, sailed out of San Diego harbor every other week. He loved his duty, his friends aboard ship, and coming home to his sweetheart. But I was miserable! Alone every other week and living in a strange city with no friends, no family, and (since I was inactive) no church affiliation, I sank often into a state of despondency. Morning sickness, nausea, and a growing waistline did not improve my attitude. I felt trapped!

At the end of each "out to sea" week, Jim would return, ever the optimist, expecting to find a happy, smiling wife. But after too many days of lonely vigilance, I was anything but sunshine. A dark gloomy cloud settled over our little rented bungalow. Doubts assailed me. I wasn't sure I loved him. He didn't seem to understand me or my needs. Was this what wedded bliss was supposed to be like? We had tried to talk it out before, but each time we satisfied only surface deficiencies.

Now we sat facing each other across the bed, our relationship teetering seriously. What were we going to do? The words *divorce* arose. Is that what we wanted? It carried a sound of finality, of permanency, and made us involuntarily shudder. But how could we change?

We sat in silence, pondering. Then Jim looked up. "Judith," he said, "I think our problem is one of selfishness. Are you willing to make an honest effort to try an experiment? For the next thirty days, I'll think only of you and your needs, and you think only of me and my needs. If at the end of that time our marriage has not improved, then we'll talk about . . . about another solution."

I agreed. I wanted—hungered for—happiness.

"But we must guard against one thing," Jim warned. "We must not predetermine each other's actions judging them against what we would like. Our wants may be out of proportion to what we receive, and disappointment may occur. This is to be a total concentration of what we can do for each other."

The next morning I slipped out of bed early, fighting nausea and bleary eyes. Jim loved large hot breakfasts; I preferred sleeping later, with a light morning snack. Nevertheless, muffins, bacon and eggs, and fruit arrived on the table. The aroma was my breakfast bell. Jim came in with a grin of eagerness that would have melted any self-serving heart. So much for sleeping in! An assortment of biscuits, ham, eggs, swedish or oven pancakes, ableskivers, and omelettes arrived on the table each morning, even though every morning I still scaled the same mountain of nausea. I purchased specialty cookbooks on breakfast meals and built up a three-week variety of different foods.

"Honey, I can hardly wait to get up in the morning just to see what exciting menu is on the table," Jim said. "You're a marvelous cook [hug and kiss], and I love it!" With this encouragement, my breakfasts continued to improve—and so did my willingness.

The second big change came during those week-long assignments out to sea. I took walks every day, started conversations with the local grocer and his wife, immersed myself in uplifting books and music, and slammed the door on every "poor me" thought. Fridays required long preparation. I knew his optimism envisioned me running out the door and into his arms—so I ran! And then I led him back into the house to discover the living room transformed by candlelight, soft music, a lace-covered card table set for dinner, and a little bit of heaven wafting from the kitchen. Romance blossomed again!

One night he said, "I feel like seeing a movie. Would you like to go?" Actually, I was tired and thinking about retiring early, but I remembered the commitment and grabbed my coat. Perhaps the hardest part is doing what you don't feel like doing, without minding. The key, I've found, is attitude. Discomfort melts to miniscule proportions under a genuine desire to please each other.

Of course I didn't do all the changing in our marriage. Jim, too, kept his part of the commitment—and he did it in ways he knew would be most meaningful to me. His largest contribution was personalized attention. Five-minute rub-downs to my aching limbs and back expanded to an hour, soothing nerves as well as body. He provided more opportunities for talk and relaxation—taking me away from our four walls on weekends into the sunshine, to the beach, or to the park for archery or picnics. And he listened more attentively to what I was feeling and going through. He perceived how easily my feelings of confidence could fail, and so he reminded me of my positive traits during those periods to bolster my ego.

Even though he was only twenty-three years old, Jim commanded one hundred men aboard ship—men who saluted and followed his orders daily. Sometimes I had suspected he unconsciously desired the same behavior from me. But, happily, during our thirty-day experiment, that harsh edge disappeared. In a matter of two weeks, I began to feel cherished, appreciated, and loved.

Our "extreme" commitment meant keeping each other's needs always in the background of our thoughts; it meant asking ourselves each day "What can I do for him/her? How can I show I care?" It meant—for both of us—literally eliminating "I demand!" and "What about me?" and "Why doesn't he/she . . . ?"

The changes in our marriage were attitudinal initially, but

they were based upon a true principle—unselfishness, and our understanding and acceptance of the principle dictated our actions. We paid the price to please each other, and in that process discovered the beginnings of true love. All it took was to give instead of take; to be thoughtful instead of thoughtless; to desire to please rather than be pleased.

About a year later, an elderly friend added his gift of wisdom to our formula: "Think of marriage as if it were an empty jar, waiting to be filled," he said. "Each act of kindness places a spoonful of sugar into it; every selfish act takes one out. At the end of each year, will your jar be empty or overflowing? Your marriage, bitter or sweet?"

Learning to be unselfish didn't mean we could relax; it required continuous effort. Warning signs were not difficult to spot, and during the years that followed we sometimes had to go back to that extreme commitment again to improve our behavior.

I remember one particular Valentine's Day with plans to dine and dance in the evening. Jim phoned from the office. "Honey, I'm sorry. We'll have to cancel. I'm tied up till late tonight." I knew he truly shared my disappointment, so after putting the children to bed, I dressed especially for him. I attached a large card to the door which read, "I Love You!" then watched for his car lights. When he walked into the house, he melted!

One evening on our anniversary, he and a dear friend Brent Brockbank, conspired together and led Kathryn (Brent's wife) and me to the backyard to find dozens of carnations, dinner, and Hawaiian music filling the warm California air. Our two husbands beamed from ear to ear.

In the spring, Jim searched the surrounding hills and found secret spots where wildflowers surfaced. "Come on," he would say. "I've got a surprise for you." And he swept me off to spend afternoons with picnic lunches amidst glorious color.

After we had been married six years, I came to a knowledge that the gospel was true. There is no question in my mind that our previous efforts to serve and please one another were at least part of the reason Jim agreed to look into the Church and allow the missionaries to come. I was reactivated, Jim was baptized, and we were sealed in the temple a year later.

The next six years sped by quickly, and our marriage continued to improve with the foundation and application of gospel principles. Little by little we dropped off the excessive, unneeded baggage that bad habits provide.

Then one night Jim returned home from an institute class and asked me about several terms he had heard there. "Do you know what these mean?" He spoke them, and they bounced against the blank wall of my mind. "I haven't the faintest idea," I answered. As we talked, a suspicion arose in us, awesome, even terrible, that we did not fully understand the doctrines of this gospel we professed to believe in—that our knowledge was shallow and unenlightened.

We started a concentrated study program immediately. We went back to the beginning again to understand faith, baptism, repentance, and the Holy Ghost. We chose vacations with the express purpose of studying together, weeks or weekends, in quiet places where we could relax, research, pray, and ponder. Growth and understanding came in sudden leaps, as well as line upon line. Our efforts again meant selflessness, sacrificing other interests occasionally, in order to keep pace with one another and to share what we learned with our family. To drag a foot was to slow the rest of us, and neither wanted to be guilty of that.

Today, gospel study and service continue to be a central activity between us, a privilege we hold most precious. As we look back, our first successes seem small now. But we will always acknowledge a certain ray of light that came one late winter evening to two desperate, seeking newlyweds. The gospel has reaffirmed to us that selflessness and service are truly a vital part of our Heavenly Father's formula for an enduring marriage.

Judith A. Long, mother of five, is a Cultural Refinement teacher in her Jacksonville Ward Relief Society. She resides in Jacksonville, Oregon.

After the Temple

We're learning to build bridges between that celestial glimpse and the rocky realities.

By Carole Osborne Cole

After enjoying the peace, the tranquility, and the great beauty of the temple, we felt sure that nothing could ever disrupt the serenity of our lives. Particularly memorable is the mental picture of our four children, clothed spotlessly in white, as they entered the room where they would be sealed to us for all eternity. Though we knew we could not remain forever in the temple, we left with a very strong desire to return and arranged for two more visits within the next forty days. Each visit was beautiful. Each time we simply did not want to leave.

But the world has a way of intruding, and as the days fled past, our feet were once more plodding earthly paths and our brief contact with heaven was just a memory. Suddenly my husband and I were in an argument, the cause so trivial and unimportant it is hardly worth remembering. But all at once I felt trapped, locked in, and completely unsure of myself. Why? After tempers had cooled, both my husband and I realized the argument was symptomatic of something far more important than the triviality, and we talked it out. We concluded the problem involved several factors:

1. After the high level of spirituality we had achieved, there

was a natural letdown which could be compared to the very real "blues" a woman often experiences after the birth of a child. There was a sudden void when our goal of fifteen years had been achieved. Deep spiritual experiences such as our visits to the temple, with the following relaxing of tension, seemed to play havoc with my emotional and spiritual equilibrium.

2. For years before his conversion, I had always had the support and help of my husband not only with my own Church work but with the household as well. He was never above lending a hand with cooking and baking, or even heavy scrubbing and window cleaning, and he was frequently our baby-sitter. But now Jim was a very conscientious home teacher, a Sunday School teacher, and then a Scoutmaster, a member of the Ward Finance Committee, and actively engaged in building fund projects. The free time he had once had to help me was now more than filled by his commitments to the Church. I also had Church work to do in addition to keeping up the home. Jim needed help in locating scriptures, having special handouts typed for his Sunday School class, and general support with his growing testimony.

3. Financially, we were committed to a heavy building fund assessment, tithing, ward budget and welfare obligations, and a large chunk for accumulation of food storage. The budget had been stretched to near the breaking point. The children's music lessons had to be cut from weekly to twice monthly. We were thrown back ten years to scrimping and scraping and living from paycheck to paycheck.

4. Maritally, Jim and I seemed to be going in different directions. We knew we shared the same goals, but our time together was reduced to a few moments' chat before bedtime, and we were often too tired for that.

5. I doubted my ability to live all I had promised. The enormity of the task of perfecting myself seemed more than I could handle. Could I ever become selfless enough to earn the celestial kingdom? Would the rest of our lives be a financial struggle? Was it wrong to want time and money for myself? Church meetings became too routine; the speakers often seemed boring and ill-prepared. Enduring to the end loomed as incredible. I had lost all perspective.

Contributing to the partial loss of spirituality was my

feeling of *giving* constantly, with very little coming back. I seemed to be continually giving to the children, my husband, the Church, and home. I was losing my life in service to others all right, but where was the life I was thus supposed to find?

Then came a call from our elders quorum president. He requested a final meeting of our temple preparation group. Four couples had taken the class, and we had all been through the temple. But he felt the need for some additional comments. My husband encouraged our attendance, over my objections.

Sensing there were problems developing among the eight of us, he began by recalling his own thoughts and attitudes after his family had been sealed in the temple. He felt lost, floundering—after the temple, what? Where do you go from there? The celestial kingdom is still a long way off. Comments from other class members reinforced his suspicion that several of us were having problems. The spiritual sensitivity of our elders quorum president was marvelous, and we listened intently.

Holding up the article, "Accepted of the Lord: The Doctrine of Making Your Calling and Election Sure," by Roy W. Doxey (*Ensign*, July 1976, p. 50), he read, "Although the process of obtaining exaltation continues even into the spirit world, the knowledge that one will become exalted . . . *can be certain in this life.*"

The realization that there were definite intermediary goals between the temple and the celestial kingdom began to bring things back into perspective. We read the full article and found comfort and assurance. There was no *less* to do, but knowing others were struggling too and that there were those in our ward who were sensitive to our needs was reassuring. After we identified our problem areas, we knew that our next step was to find solutions and set goals.

Depression. Simple recognition of the factors involved in our period of instability after our sealing in the temple also helped us put things in the proper light. As a woman I could relate to those "after-the-baby" blues, and I felt relief in realizing I was feeling a release of tensions after such an uplifting experience. It was a natural reaction to a very special, long-anticipated event.

Time and money. A direct look at the covenants we had

made prompted the answer to the next two problem areas—having less time and money. Had we not promised the Lord *all* our time, talent, and financial means if he should need them? Had we meant what we promised? Of course, our family's exaltation is worth whatever price we have to pay—in time, money, and talent. The memory of those four children in the sealing room was reassurance of that.

Financially, we accepted the fact that we might be in a bind for a while. Before Jim's conversion, he steadfastly argued that tithing or not, two and two cannot make five. Though at the moment we seem not to have a dime to spare, we can look back over the year since going to the temple and see what has been accomplished. We bought a car, met our building fund and all other assessments, paid a full tithe, gathered a year's supply of food, sent a daughter off to Ricks College, purchased an insurance policy that will assure our two sons money enough for missions when they are of age, took a two-week trip to California, and even got away as husband and wife to Canada for four days—something we've never been able to manage before. In addition, we have plans to build the house we've always wanted—and all still on the same salary (plus a cost-of-living raise) we were making before the temple! Jim was right—two and two cannot make five. When you put the Lord first, two and two make six!

Time for each other. Perhaps the most important realization came when we recognized that a good part of our difficulty stemmed from our failure to spend more time with each other. Being sealed in the temple for all eternity does not eliminate the need for talking and listening to each other, laughing and crying together, and generally nourishing a marriage. How easy it is to lose touch with one another! How quickly grow the seeds of discontent when there is not time to talk over problems, accomplishments, hopes, and daily observations! Our answer was to set aside Friday evening as our special time. Just as Monday is family night, Friday is husband and wife night. We may choose to attend a ward function, or we may feel the need to be alone. We may talk, drive, walk, play tennis, window shop, see a movie—but it is our time to be together. Just as the dating and courting period serves a very real purpose of helping a couple get to know each other, so do special husband and wife dates serve a very real purpose in assuring that we continue to know one another and grow together. We *make* the time for one another that is necessary for our marriage to be the vital, growing, lively contact we need to be happy.

Spirituality. There are any number of ways to feed ourselves spiritually. Basic, of course, is attendance at Sunday meetings. Partaking of the sacrament is necessary to spirituality. Individual scripture study, fasting and prayer, education days or weeks, reading books by General Authorities, and keeping a journal are all ways to keep our spirituality viable and the motivating force it should be in our lives. Jim and I feast spiritually from a visit to the temple. Being fortunate enough to live within four hours' drive of a temple prompted our decision to attend at least once every two to three months. When we leave after one visit, we immediately look forward to the next. When we know we will be coming back soon, it isn't quite so hard to leave.

Time for one's self. The identity crisis used to be, in my opinion, a handy catch-all phrase. But I've come to realize we must all go through such a "crisis" in order to recognize our place as husbands and wives, as fathers and mothers in our families as well as in the Church. Until we come to grips with our roles in these various areas, we will never be thoroughly content with much of anything we do.

The question of how much to contribute to family, Church work, profession, and other obligations is one that is likely to be most difficult to analyze. After a woman gives her best to the various roles involved in being wife, mother, daughter of God, how much time, if any, is left for other interests? After a man gives his best to *his* various roles, how much of his time is left over?

Of course, one of the beauties of the gospel is that we can develop our talents and find personal satisfaction and growth through the many programs of the Church. Creative talents are encouraged and utilized in music, dance, drama, and in the many Church positions that require the development of leadership and teaching abilities. Study of the gospel itself is a lifelong educational opportunity. But whether my individual interest is Church-related or not, for my own mental health, I need something of my very own. Part of my need is filled through keeping a personal journal. Writing about my thoughts and feelings helps me keep a proper perspective in all areas of my life.

The mother who builds her entire life around her children may be left empty when they grow to maturity and begin their own lives. The wife who has no life outside her husband's interests may run the risk of smothering their relationship and bringing only her *needs* to their lives rather than making a contribution in her own right. The husband who is a "workaholic" will probably find his wife and children have little interest in him in later years.

Putting just the right amount of energy and devotion into each of our roles in life is the art we need to develop in the years between the temple and the end of our mortal path. It means establishing priorities. In order to get to the temple we had to attend our meetings, pay a full tithe, keep morally clean, be honest, sustain the authorities, etc. After the temple, enduring to the end was added to the list. So after the temple comes the time to organize ourselves, to nourish ourselves, to grow to maturity spiritually, mentally, and emotionally in preparation for a place in our Father's kingdom.

Carole Osborne Cole is currently serving as a Cultural Refinement teacher in the Bountiful Thirty-ninth Ward Relief Society and is the mother of four children.

Let's Help This Marriage Grow!

The marital relationship is much like raising a beautiful flower. You nourish it with a wise and loving balance of necessary ingredients.

By James M. Harper

A young woman sat across from me describing what seemed to her to be a "hopeless" marriage. She had been married in the temple only a few short months before, but things just weren't working out. The romance was disappearing, she said; her attraction to her husband had been lost in the daily responsibilities of living. When I asked why he hadn't come with her, she replied that he didn't see any problem in their relationship. "He's really a good man," she said, "but I'm just not committed to him anymore. My love is gone."

I have thought many times since that day about commitment in marriage. The Savior taught the principle of commitment when he answered the Pharisees, saying, "For this cause shall a man leave father and mother, and shall cleave to his wife. . . . What therefore God hath joined together, let not man put asunder." (Matthew 19:5-6.) The word *cleave* is a powerful action word meaning to adhere closely.

Love is the necessary ingredient in cleaving to one's spouse. "Thou shalt love thy wife with all thy heart," the Lord said, "and shalt cleave unto her and none else." (D&C 42:22.) However, the term *love* has different meanings to different people. To some, love is only an emotional and physical attraction accompanied by romantic idealization. To them, love doesn't necessarily include the important concepts of commitment and cleaving. To others, love is the quiet, steady feeling that develops between people when they share important life experiences. Both kinds of love are important; both contribute to good marriages. But in many cases, romantic love is overplayed, while the commitment that leads to true cleaving is lacking.

As a young missionary in the Republic of South Korea, I was impressed with the quality of many of the Korean people's marriages. When I was told that the marriages were arranged by parents, I wondered how two people could cleave so well without having first developed romantic love toward each other. Because of the narrow view I had at the time of commitment in marriage, I thought romantic feelings were the sole binding force.

But I learned some basic principles about committed love as I observed those marriages. I learned that when two people work with each other to produce a home, when they struggle to keep children fed and healthy—then love occurs. When illness or adversity strikes and one spouse sacrifices to help and care for the other—then they learn to love. When husband and wife are progressing together spiritually and emotionally—then love grows. Love, I learned, comes as the marriage, and the marriage partners, develop.

How then can a married couple foster commitment to each other?

1. In Times of Crisis, Pull Together

Crises can build strong marriages. It is unfortunate that some couples see struggles in marriage as an excuse to escape. Too often they fall into blaming each other for the stresses rather than relying on each other for affection and support. Trials in life can serve as a foundation to committed love.

Recently my wife and children were very ill from an unusual bacterial infection. I gave them blessings and prayed for them. Then, not wanting to expose anyone else to their sickness, I arranged my work schedule to be able to be home to care for their needs. It was soon apparent that my acts of service to help them through three weeks of illness became a strong binding force for us. Such struggles in life sometimes push marital partners apart, but crises can serve as the training ground for commitment. We often perform such acts of service because we are committed beforehand, but in many instances *service precedes commitment.* It is in serving each other that we become committed to each other.

The marital relationship is much like raising rare, beautiful flowers. You plant the seed and nourish it with water, food, soil, and light. If the delicate balance of these ingredients is upset, the growth and beauty of the flower may be disturbed for a time. But working to achieve a balance of required nutrition, you can overcome the problem. Commitment to the flower comes as you take care of its needs and try to help it grow into beauty.

President Spencer W. Kimball has discussed the relationship between marital love and adversity: "A marriage may not always be even and incident-less, but it can be one of great peace," he has promised. "A couple may have poverty, illness, disappointment, failures, and even death in the family, but even these will not rob them of their peace. The marriage can be successful so long as selfishness does not enter in. Troubles and problems will draw parents together into unbreakable unions if there is total unselfishness there. During the depression of the 1930s there was a definite drop in divorce. Poverty, failures, disappointment—they tied parents together. Adversity can cement relationships that prosperity can destroy." (*Marriage & Divorce,* Salt Lake City: Deseret Book, 1976, pp. 19, 22.)

In my own marriage, I have made a very conscious decision not to let outside struggles drive me from my wife. I have learned that, besides the Lord, she is my greatest support in any crisis. If I allow fears and irritations about a problem to divide us, I have excluded the person who could best help me turn the crisis into a strength.

2. Set Common Goals

Even when a couple experiences a division between them, working toward a shared goal can revive the ties that bind them together. Too often couples negatively emphasize the differences between them. It is more important to emphasize shared aspirations and work toward them.

I learned this principle as a Boy Scout leader in a struggle to get two groups of boys to change their negative attitudes toward each other. After trying several unsuccessful strategies, I placed them in a situation which required cooperation to overcome an obstacle. They united to achieve a common goal, and we never experienced conflict between the two groups after that day.

Recently I listened as a couple complained that they had few interests in common. She liked to read; he didn't. He played raquetball, but physical problems kept her from doing so. The list of differences went on and on. I asked if there wasn't just one interest they shared. They shook their heads. Finally I suggested they take a ceramics class together. Neither had tried anything like that, so it gave them a new common interest. The effect was unbelievable. As they worked toward a common goal, the excitement of growing together helped them gradually forget their differences.

3. Seek Ways to Nurture Your Spouse

It would be wise for all of us to ask the following question frequently: "What have I done recently to improve my spouse's feelings about himself or herself?" By deciding to enhance one another's self-esteem, we become very committed to each other; the other's improvement in the way they feel becomes our success as well. In addition, we need to be willing to help our partners grow in whatever area they might desire. Spouses need to encourage each other in spiritual pursuits, intellectual development, and physical fitness. It is important to encourage them, rather than discourage them by nagging remarks and demands. When we accept the goal of helping our spouse grow in a chosen area, we will experience the commitment to that person which accompanies such an attitude.

Nurturing also means finding strengths rather than weaknesses in our spouse. One of the recurring differences in studies of happily married couples compared to marriages in trouble is the amount of positive daily conversation. A good rule is to make at least two-thirds of our conversations with our spouse pleasant, positive, and nurturing to both. Problems need to be talked about and worked through, but to spend all of our time together solving problems isn't appealing in any relationship.

4. Learn to Love Yourself

"He that loveth his wife loveth himself. For no man ever yet hated his own flesh; but nourisheth it and cherisheth it." (Ephesians 5:28-29.) It is extremely difficult to be committed to our husband or wife when we feel we have nothing to offer. Just as we can't focus primarily on our spouse's weaknesses, we should strive to give positive messages to ourselves.

We sometimes have degrading conversations within ourselves. Listening to the thoughts and feelings that enter our minds when we look in the mirror, meet someone for the first time, or complete a task can be a key in determining the degree of love we have for ourselves. Replacing negative thoughts with positive ones can increase our self-love. Another assignment that has benefitted many individuals is to imagine themselves behaving in successful and positive ways.

5. Strive to Always Be Open to New Understandings about Your Spouse

We never know all there is to discover about anyone. Even though we may be married to someone for a lifetime, that someone is growing and changing. This fact makes marriage exciting—there are always delightful new things to learn about our spouse if we search for them.

One husband was recently astonished at the depth of his wife's knowledge about political candidates. She had studied the issues and analyzed each candidate's stand. He gained a new respect for her in his attempts to learn from her study. Another couple spends time sharing the books each reads. The husband doesn't have as much time to read, but he enjoys sharing what she reads. The nicest part is that he learns a great deal about his wife's values and feelings through their discussions. This keeps their marriage vibrant and stimulating.

6. Give Your Marriage Top Priority

Some parents become closer to their children than to each

other. Children might even try to get one parent to side with them against the other. When this occurs, it does not help the child or the parents. Likewise, people and activities outside the family can have a stronger hold on us than our wives or husbands. Work, leisure, and friends can interfere with the strength of the marital commitment. It is important to guard against this by planning and taking time to talk and be together as a couple.

7. Renew Events That Symbolize Your Marriage

Anniversaries are significant events because they symbolize the marital commitment. Other events and places associated with the marriage or courtship can also become symbolic. By renewing acts such as giving flowers, writing notes, or observing special celebrations, couples are reminded of their bond. Some couples plan a time when they can leave the children with a competent babysitter for a weekend and get away. These practices serve to strengthen "cleaving together."

At a very young age I realized my father and mother loved each other very much. Their anniversary was an event marked with great celebration. The look on my mother's face when my father presented her with a dozen red roses is indelibly painted in my mind. On my own wedding day, we also selected roses to represent our special occasion—thus we continued a tradition that symbolized commitment and love.

8. Make the Gospel the Foundation of Your Marriage

Celestial living involves a never ending marital commitment. The life that results from obedience to gospel principles is one of service and compassion to one's spouse and family. When a man and woman are married for eternity, they decide that they can better progress spiritually together than either could alone. The temple marriage does not promise to erase the struggles of married life, but it does offer the potential for commitment that can be achieved in no other way.

James M. Harper, a professor in marriage and family therapy, Brigham Young University, and father of four, is currently serving as mission president of the Korea Pusan Mission.

SHOWING LOVE AND AFFECTION

Keeping Your Marriage Alive

No marriage will fail—no matter how long the couple has been married—if each partner seriously strives to enrich the marriage on a continual basis.

By Paul E. Dahl

The voice on the telephone said, "Paul, I must see you as soon as possible. My wife and I are having problems in our marriage." We made an appointment for later that day, and as I put down the telephone, I felt shocked and concerned. Here, I had thought, was a solid marriage. What could have gone wrong?

There were several possible factors, including stress over financial matters, but after my discussions with Bill and Sharon (not their real names), I found that the failure to develop and continually maintain a good husband/wife relationship was central. As we talked, I concluded that they were both doing adequate jobs in their roles as father and mother, but that they hadn't spent enough time and effort on their own relationship.

In their twenty years of marriage, Bill and Sharon had usually included others in their activities, especially their children. But very seldom did just the two of them spend time together. They emphasized children's birthdays, but not each other's. When Christmas arrived, most of the gifts were for the children; this was also true of other occasions during the year. Yes, they were involved as parents, but they were neglecting each other. Even when they went to dinner it was always with another couple. And when Bill expressed his feelings about Sharon's personal grooming, she responded, "There was never enough time or money after providing for the children's needs!" She then expressed feelings of being ignored and never really feeling important in her husband's eyes. "In fact," she stated, "I have felt just like another one of the children. Everything has been planned to meet their needs." Humbled, Bill admitted: "I have heard so much through the years about the importance of being a father, that I apparently have forgotten how to be a husband."

At this point, I felt it was appropriate to share a statement made by one of my influential teachers. He said that no couple can meet their full potential as parents until they have first developed a strong husband-and-wife relationship. Bill and Sharon agreed with this and acknowledged that they both had much to learn about being good marriage partners. They also felt empathy for another couple who, the morning after the last child was married, came to breakfast, and as they looked at each other across the table, found they had nothing to talk about.

Bill and Sharon realized that they needed to do something immediately to avoid a trend to divorce. They had a strong desire to strengthen their marriage and quickly took steps to develop their relationship. Together, they accepted and worked on the following specific assignments:

Assignment 1: *Strengthen Your Relationship with Our Father in Heaven.*

Remember that Heavenly Father can soften hearts, soothe hurt feelings, and bless a couple with the ability to forgive past mistakes. He can help husbands and wives draw closer to each other, increase their communication skills, and magnify their understanding and love.

Sometimes couples are too embarrassed to share spiritual feelings with each other. Or they get so busy with other things that they don't make time for this crucial part of their relationship. I counseled Bill and Sharon to pray together daily and to study together the scriptures and recent talks from the General Authorities. I encouraged them to make discussion and testimony bearing a part of these sessions.

Assignment 2: Spend Time Alone Together.

I had learned by personal experience the importance of time alone with my wife. With the beginning of a new school year, student conferences, opening socials, and upcoming stake and general conferences, September is always a hectic month for our family. Several years ago I spent four successive weekends away from home, and I was behind with many household and yard chores. The first free Saturday found me doing some needed chores at my workbench (and really feeling good about getting caught up) when I was surprised by a knock on the door. There stood my wife, and she stated with much conviction, "I just want to let you know I've got to get away and I'm leaving now. If you want to come, fine; but I'm going."

Well, I may not be the most intelligent person in the world, but I understood the message. I left my now no-longer-important project and escorted her straight to the car. "Let's have a picnic—all alone," I suggested, and we stopped by a convenience market to buy some sunflower seeds, yogurt, and fruit juice. A strange picnic? Not when we *both* liked this combination of items. We drove to a national monument a few minutes from our home, and under the pleasant, fall Arizona sunshine enjoyed a memorable picnic. We included a short hike, talked about the two of us, and enjoyed one of the most eventful afternoons of our life. It didn't cost much and we didn't go very far, but it accomplished the needed renewal: we spent some time alone.

I shared this experience with Bill and Sharon and was happy that each succeeding week Bill reported on their "dates" together. He discovered that a date could be simple and inexpensive, like taking a walk, going on a picnic (even without yogurt and sunflower seeds), taking a drive, watching the sunset, going to dinner, eating at home (when the children were out), or shopping together.

This couple made an effort to share time together. It did take extra planning, especially in finding someone to watch the children for them. Neither Bill nor Sharon had family living near them, so they located a neighbor willing to watch the children for a few hours (occasionally overnight) in return for a similar favor. But the rewards were well worth the planning. They were able to create the time they needed. As Clayton C. Barbeau states: "I have never yet stumbled across twenty minutes lying on the sidewalk, though once I found a twenty-dollar bill. Nor have I ever met anyone who just happened across two weeks of time somebody had left in the park. I doubt that anyone else has done so either, for the simple reason that time is not found." (*Creative Marriage*, New York: Seabury Press, 1976, p. 75.)

Bill and Sharon planned each week to include more and more of the things they both secretly had long yearned to do together. Time was also allotted for the children, and they continued to have activities as an entire family on a regular basis.

Assignment 3: Listen to Each Other.

For years Sharon had been trying to express to Bill her special needs; in turn, he had been attempting to communicate his feelings regarding her appearance. But neither had had "ears" for the other. I asked them to take thirty minutes each day during these critical weeks to listen. They decided that late evening, just before retiring, was the most convenient time for them. I asked them to take turns expressing something positive about the other person and then wait for the response. Building upon that base of appreciation, each was then to discuss one frustration they felt concerning their mate, but in very loving terms, again taking turns and awaiting a response. As their confidence increased, they were willing to discuss lovingly some feelings they had been carrying for years, and they thus developed a trust they had previously never known. This time together was so rewarding that it became a regular habit.

One of the important results of this experience has been that they now regularly discuss their budget. This has reduced the strain between them created by misinformation about the family's financial affairs. Both understand how much money can be spent, and together they decide how it is to be spent.

Assignment 4: Develop a Friendship with Your Spouse.

Recently a woman in our town, who had been a wife for forty-two years, stated that she and her husband were "terribly good friends" and had a tremendous amount of respect for each other. She said this greatly strengthened their relationship because they always had something to talk about. They understood each other and were interested in each other. Too often we think that friendships are something external to marriage, but it is my experience that a really happy and healthy marriage is based on a solid friendship. Eventually, Bill and Sharon developed a strong friendship—the result of taking time to recognize each other's unsatisfied needs and then working together to fulfill them.

Assignment 5: *Do Something Special for the Other Person Every Day.*

Many marriages terminate because one or both of the partners take the other for granted. The marriage gets lost in the woodwork of life, with each person becoming involved in his or her own interests. The wife too often spends all of her time caring for the children. The husband may become totally immersed in his work. Sometimes church callings and other activities consume all of one's extra time. In such a situation, the image of the other spouse becomes almost invisible against the background of the busy environment.

This couple was a classic example. In fact, they were so far apart in meeting each other's needs that they did not know where to begin. As they commenced talking, they were very cautious. For example, Sharon said, "If I baked you a pecan pie, would that be something special?"

Bill exclaimed, "Would that be special! You've never baked a pecan pie. You've always felt we couldn't afford it." Then he asked, "Would it be special if I took you to the stake sweetheart dance next week?"

She started to cry and said, "I didn't think we would ever go to a dance again."

Sharon was elated with little gifts from her "new" sweetheart during the subsequent weeks. And she supplied basketball tickets for the two of them so they could attend a game that was special to Bill. Most important, however, was Sharon's asking Bill to share with her what he really did at his job. She had never before shown an interest.

Too often we equate doing things for others as something that will cost considerable money. I well remember my first Valentine's Day with my wife. We had been married just six weeks. I was attending school and was a typical struggling student with no extra money. Having a desire to please my new bride, I took the $1.25 I had and went to the florist for two daffodils, to the candy shop for a small box of chocolates, and then to the drugstore for a valentine. I placed them on our small living room table, and when my wife returned from work you would have thought she had received a dozen long-stemmed roses, a two-pound box of chocolates, and the world's largest valentine. The next year was somewhat different—after all, we had then been married over a year! I neglected to purchase a remembrance. The disappointment was obvious—so obvious in fact, that during the last twenty-eight years I have not forgotten a Valentine's Day, birthday, or anniversary.

Sometimes couples think they get too old to do special things for each other and to express appreciation. But age doesn't have to present a barrier. An en excellent example comes from Mrs. Edwin R. (Mary) Firmage, the daughter of President and Sister Hugh B. Brown, who shared the following regarding the marriage of her parents in their later years:

"Up until Mother's stroke they'd go through a ritual daily. Daddy would get up from the breakfast table that Mother had set very nicely, with a pretty cloth, matching napkins, and flowers. He'd kiss her good-bye and then they would walk to the front porch together. Daddy would go down three steps, and then turn around and ask, 'Did I kiss you good-bye?' Mother would answer, 'Why, no, you didn't.' Daddy would kiss her again.

"As he walked to the car, Mother would run into the dining room where she would blow kisses to him from the window. While Daddy was backing the car out of the drive, Mother would run back to the porch where she'd wave a handkerchief until he drove out of sight. Just before the car turned the corner, Daddy would blink the brake lights three times, his code for 'I love you.' " (*Church News*, 26 Oct. 1974, p. 5.)

These are the kinds of "little" things that keep a marriage alive.

Assignment 6: *Share with Your Spouse Those Things in Your Marriage That Have Been Most Meaningful to You.*

A very effective exercise to help develop communication is to list the positive experiences from your marriage that you remember best. For practical purposes, limit each list to twenty items. This will help to identify those areas in the marriage that have been most meaningful. In making the list, make only brief statements. For example: 1. Our honeymoon, 2. When you surprised me on my birthday, 3. When we walked together along the beach. Then find adequate time to share the lists. Discuss each event and why it was meaningful. Make plans to see that more of the same happens.

When Bill and Sharon took time to use this simple exercise, they were surprised to find there were really more positive events in their marriage than they had ever realized.

Assignment 7: *Take a Second (or Third or Fourth) Honeymoon.*

Bill and Sharon needed a second honeymoon—to find themselves exclusively in the role of a married couple, unhindered by the presence of children, friends, or relatives. Every couple needs, on a regular basis, to escape the myriad of roles expected of them, to savor nothing but a husband-and-wife relationship in a setting that each enjoys. This honeymoon may last only one day or involve a short trip, but it does mean getting away from family and acquaintances—and especially the telephone.

A bishop's wife once confirmed this by stating that the survival of her marriage depended on these rendezvous with her husband several times a year, usually just traveling across town to a motel. Some of our acquaintances go camping on their "honeymoon" since they *both* enjoy the outdoors. It certainly should be a situation where both husband and wife can relax and share the entire experience. A honeymoon is not the husband playing golf while the wife remains at the hotel reading her favorite book. It must be a sharing experience. Bill and Sharon spent a weekend "honeymoon" and were overjoyed with the experience.

Assignment 8: *Share a New Experience.*

It has been said that one of the basic needs of mankind is new experiences. I have found marriages must also have new experiences. They need to be redecorated periodically with fresh activities just as we redecorate our homes. Several years ago I was made aware of an older couple who always had bread, milk, and cheese for their evening meal. As I observed their relationship, it was obvious to me that their marriage was no more exciting than their routine supper menu. Marriages can get into ruts, and the ruts grow deeper and deeper over the years.

Couples need to do new things continually to expand their boundaries. Travel, try a new hobby together, work together on creative projects. There are many activities that can be shared. Bill and Sharon decided to take up dancing. Although they were both interested in dancing, they had never taken the time to enjoy this activity. They took lessons and thoroughly enjoyed their new, shared experience. Other couples have taken up such activities as golf, bowling, rock hunting, eating new foods, cooking, and taking adult education classes.

Happily, Bill and Sharon were able to heal the crack that had developed in their marriage. They learned, as Paul said, that "neither is the man without the woman, neither the woman without the man, in the Lord." (1 Corinthians 11:11.)

Their completeness was restored as they shared once more their sacred roles and learned that it can be a great joy to be husband and wife. They became aware that no marriage will fail—no matter how long the couple has been married—if each partner seriously strives to enrich the marriage on a continual basis.

Paul E. Dahl, director of the Cambridge Institute of Religion, and father of five, serves as Young Men's president and Family Relations instructor in his Arlington, Massachusetts, ward.

The Best Gift

The image of the three of us with those giant potatoes became one of my cherished memories.

By Jennie L. Hansen

I'm not sure why that day was so special; I only know that I often find myself recalling it vividly. I can still feel the warm wind blowing on my skin, the thick mud between my toes, a strand of dirty white hair in my mouth. And the love.

Daddy was participating in an experimental project for the Idaho Extension Service. He was one of those first farmers to raise the "certified" potato seed which would eventually make Idaho world-famous for its quality baking potatoes. That particular day he came in from the fields to get Mama in the middle of the day. He talked her into lugging along her big black box camera. My sister and I tagged along as they walked to the far side of the north field.

When Daddy turned to walk down one of the deep furrows, MarJean and I each started down furrows of our own. We carefully scanned each lush green plant for the slightest trace of yellow. After all, *we* knew how to "rogue" potatoes.

Part way down the row Daddy stooped, and with the flat of his hand began to burrow in the ground beneath a large thick potato vine. There he unearthed the biggest potatoes any of us had ever seen. A grin spread over his face, and his eyes shone as

Mama took snapshots of him with half-a-dozen huge spuds resting in his hands and on his arms. Then she took pictures of my sister and me holding the giant potatoes. I sat in the furrow and made mud bricks, carefully shaping each little square with my fingers until they were as perfect as the miniature bricks Grandma kept at her house for us to play with when we visited. Every once in a while I would glance up to see Daddy with his arm around Mama's shoulder, his hand lightly gripping the top of her arm. They smiled and talked. I demolished my brick house before we left so it wouldn't dam up the water the next time Daddy irrigated.

That night Daddy came in from watering while Mama was still washing dishes. I knew he was going to tease her because he had that look on his face. With his hands behind his back, he sneaked up behind her. She really jumped and I giggled when he thrust a bouquet of wildflowers into her arms. He often brought her flowers: dark purple violets, delicate lady slippers, sweet-smelling pale pink roses, and feathery lavendar daisies.

Years later, as a teenager, I ran across the snapshots my mother had taken that day. I was so dirty and ragged! My wispy white hair looked as though it had never known a comb. Shocked, I wondered why I remembered that day as one of the happiest of my life, when I had obviously looked like one of Dickens's street urchins.

It was not until several more years had passed that a glimmer of understanding came to me when I read the words of Reverend Theodore Hesburgh, who wrote: "The most important thing a father can do for his children is to love their mother." (*Reader's Digest*, Jan. 1963, p. 25.) At that moment I understood how a single day, bathed in the love of parents for each other, could be one of the greatest gifts of childhood.

Jennie L. Hansen is the mother of five children and serves as Cultural Refinement leader in the Hunter Second Ward. She resides in West Valley City, Utah.

"Really, Is It Any Wonder I Love Her?"

How Husbands and Wives Show Their Love for Each Other

By Marvin K. Gardner

It was late and the house was dark when she got home. Freezing and exhausted after chaperoning a Mutual snow party (where she had melted the toes of her boots over the campfire), Barbara Yates of Blackfoot, Idaho, tiptoed into her bedroom, thinking her husband was asleep. To her surprise she found the bed untouched, a bag of marshmallows on her pillow, and a certificate from her husband (effective immediately) good for a warm bath, a clean towel, and a cup of hot chocolate.

When Karen Schiffman's husband asked her to lunch one Friday afternoon, she accepted, believing his story about finding a new spot a few minutes away from their home in Orem, Utah. But when he picked her up, he drove to the freeway and headed north, speeding past the exits. The farther they went, the more questions she asked and the bigger her husband's grin grew. Finally he turned to her and asked: "How would you like lunch in Salt Lake City—oh, and dinner and breakfast, too?"

Karen just stared at him with her mouth open. They'd left their four children with a friend for just a short luncheon date. But he explained that he had arranged for a babysitter, packed the suitcases, and reserved a motel room "for a much needed overnight vacation."

When the *Ensign* asked husbands and wives how they show their love for each other, answers were received from thirty states, seven countries, and a couple of APO and "at sea" addresses. Some were very similar, varying only slightly. Others were more creative. But when all the answers are seen as a group, it becomes obvious that love is abundant in many Latter-day Saint marriages, and that even though it is expressed in hundreds of ways, it is recognized, relished, and reciprocated.

Not at all startling is the repeated idea that the feelings aren't expressed in dramatic or spectacular displays. Usually they are a result of days and years and lifetimes of quiet words and moments, sensitivity and selflessness, spiritual support—and a great deal of thoughtfulness.

Quiet Words and Moments

Why is it that the words "I love you"—when said to the right person, by the right person, at the right moment—are so important? Yet according to the letters, that well-used phrase in never overused. Officiators in every Latter-day Saint temple in the world counsel thousands of newlyweds every year to express their love for each other daily—to come right out and say it. "If your husband doesn't tell you every day that he loves you," some jokingly instruct the bride, "you come back and tell me about it!"

"I've never had to go back and complain," says Laura Irwin of Dawson Creek, British Columbia. "And in eight years he's never forgotten our anniversary, either. Maybe that's because it's on April Fools' Day!"

Of course there is an infinite number of ways to say "I love you." But the Saints who responded to the survey unanimously agree that those other ways should accompany, not replace, the actual words—that daily expressions of love are a wonderful reminder.

Arlene Pommerville of Midland, Michigan, says her husband frequently asks her if she'll marry him again. "I thought he was just being silly," Arlene says, "so I never thought too much about it." But after realizing that some couples probably wouldn't marry each other again, she began to look forward to hearing his request. "I am glad that after nine children and fourteen years of marriage he would still ask me to be his eternal companion all over again."

One Salt Lake City woman says that although her husband wasn't very demonstrative, his "goodnight, sweetheart" and kiss "always made me feel loved and cherished." He said it almost every night until his death.

Wives know they need to be expressive, too. It's not uncommon for them to meet their husbands at the door with a hug and a kiss. Although May Nielson of Payson, Utah, usually didn't do that sort of thing in the middle of the day, she tried it once when her husband came in from the fields at noon. "He looked a bit surprised," she says, but they both liked it so much that they've made it a habit. "We didn't need anything like this to assure each other of our love," she explains. "But it has been like an extra bonus, an enrichment of our already happy companionship."

Short phone calls once a day from their husbands are very popular with many wives, especially young mothers who feel they need at least one "sane" conversation during the day. Love poetry is also popular, as well as "I love you" in sign language. And three anythings—squeezes of the hand, light taps on the shoulder, horn honks when driving away, or blinks of the headlights—symbolize "I love you" to some. When Gertrude Blair of LaCrescenta, California, stood by her husband's hospital bed during emergency treatment for a cardiac arrest, she took his hand, felt three faint squeezes, and told the doctors that he would be all right. Within moments her husband's heartbeat again registered on the monitor screen.

Writing love notes isn't really a new idea, but it's not a stale one, either, according to the letters the *Ensign* received. Such notes are found all over Latter-day Saint homes, in lunch boxes, in shirt pockets, in shoes, on the refrigerator, in scriptures, in overnight cases. Afterwards, they're found in scrapbooks and other repositories of family treasures.

Brent Arnell, a Scoutmaster from Calabasas, California, found notes placed in several strategic spots in his pack at summer camp. "Sorry you hurt yourself," said the note in the Band-Aid box. And in his razor, which he didn't use until the last day, he found: "I'm so glad you decided to shave before coming home. See you this afternoon!"

Sally Gale of Layton, Utah, writes "wisecracks" on the shells of the hard-boiled eggs she puts in her husband's lunch. The cracks run from semi-serious ("We are eggstremely proud of you") to fun. On April Fools' Day, the note said, "Want to hear a funny yolk?" When he cracked the egg, he found that it was raw.

Hoping to get a laugh and maybe a comment about putting too much sugar in her husband's lunch, Mella Bedel of Centerville, Utah, put a note inside his sandwich. But when Dan didn't say anything about it, she questioned him. His sandwich *had* seemed a little extra chewy that day, he admitted. Some sandwich-eating husbands don't get that far. LeAnn Averett of Springville, Utah, still has one note she wrote to her husband—with a bite taken out of it.

Lorraine Jones of Riverside, California, often tucks notes here and there in her husband's clean clothes. One morning he woke her up early, asking: "Don't you love me anymore? All my socks are empty!"

Husbands are note-writers, too. Mary Winters of Lemon Grove, California, finds computer-written love notes when she cleans out her husband's lunch box. One year Jean Hammond of Idaho Falls, Idaho, found twelve index cards in her Christmas stocking, each redeemable for a temple session and a treat (dinner, chocolate malt, an activity of her choice). And when Gayle Randall of Enterprise, Utah, returned home after a short visit with relatives, the notes that turned up all over the house were evidence that Theron had missed her: "Washing dishes isn't fun, Oh Dearest Darling mine! Jog my memory of this fact, And I'll take you out to dine!"

Summing up the feelings of note-writers and note-receivers, Joan Spencer of Lansing, Michigan, said, "Nothing can lift a day more than warm words of love from someone you care for."

Sensitivity and Selflessness

It's clear from the letters that husbands and wives love sensitive, understanding partners and that being that way is often the best proof of love. Traveling on a long trip was becoming "an emotional challenge" for Margie Johnson of Provo, Utah, because her three energetic children under five were tired of being cooped up in the car for so long. Noticing this, Jim, who usually drives, pulled over and offered to change places. "It would have been much easier for him to keep driving and try to ignore the baby," Margie says, "but he knew that I enjoyed driving and needed a reprieve. His consideration for my feelings plays a big part in our marriage."

When the doctor told a California woman that she might never have children, she "spent the whole evening enveloped in a cloud of self-pity and gloom, angry that I had to carry such an unfair burden." But when her husband arrived home, he handed her a paper bag containing two bottles of her favorite colognes. To some, she explains, that might have been the wrong gift for that particular moment. But he was sensitive enough to her feelings to know that the gift was just right for her. "I realized that this was his quiet way of letting me know that he loved me, and that our problem didn't diminish my womanliness to him in any way."

Taci Fernuik of Amarillo, Texas, was so excited about her first Halloween after she was married that she went all out to decorate their little apartment and make special treats for the trick-or-treaters. But it got later and later and not *one* masked youngster wandered down the dark driveway to the back of the house and then down the stairs to their basement apartment. As every uneventful half-hour ticked away, she became more depressed. Finally her husband, Ron, put on his coat and left. He returned a few minutes later without telling her where he had gone. But just then Taci heard some giggling outside the door. The doorbell rang, and "trick-or-treat!" echoed in her ears.

Another form of sensitivity is selflessness—the willingness to put the other person first, to make sacrifices for each other and the family. And equally important is appreciation for that selflessness.

Many wives say they appreciate the way their husbands fulfill their role as husbands and fathers. "He shows he loves me," several write, "by spending so much time with me and the children." "Knowing how much he cares for and loves our children brings me great honor and a feeling of self-worth," says Linda Cox of Goldsboro, North Carolina. Most husbands understand that their wives who stay at home don't get to punch out at five o'clock and leave everything until the next day. And they understand, too, that whether their wives work at home or away from home they are usually as tired by the time evening comes as men are. Many husbands see evenings and weekends as a joint responsibility with their wives, rather than just hers alone.

A typical example of this was found in a letter from Faye Sowards of San Jose, California. When she was first married, Faye worked in a bank while her husband also worked and went to school. Trying to be very organized about her housework, she sorted out a basketful of laundry one morning to wash later on when she got home. But when she returned that evening, she found that her husband, eager to do his part, had helped—he had *ironed* the whole basket of dirty clothes! He got more into the hang of things later on, Faye says. After their first baby was born, he would get up in the night, change the diaper, and bring the baby to her for nursing. "The novelty of this system didn't wear off even through five pregnancies," she says. "I know our three sons will be considerate husbands and fathers," she continues, reflecting the thoughts of a multitude of other wives, "because they have had such a terrific live-in model. I recognize how fortunate I am and try to show him how much I appreciate all he does for me."

Some husbands completely take over the care of the house and the kids for one evening a week so their wives can have some quiet time to themselves. Husbands recognize and appreciate their wives' efforts and selflessness, too. Typical is the response of Steve Thornbrue of Portland, Oregon, who says his wife shows her love by filling their home with laughter and music, making it a place of simple elegance and cleanliness, and caring so devotedly for their children. And Bryan Gordon of Blackfoot, Idaho, says that it is "pleasant to think during the day of going home where peace and love are waiting."

Spiritual Support

Sharing things of the spirit with each other, working side by side to achieve mutual and personal goals, experiencing testimony and good feelings and peace—all of these things draw husbands and wives closer together and increase their love for one another. Taci Fernuik, expressing the thoughts of many others, says her husband "evidences love for me every time he leads the family in scripture reading, prayers, and family home evening. But something extra special to me is his evidence of love when he lays his hands on my head and blesses me to get well. I'm so thankful for a man like this, and am striving to be worthy of him."

Paige Reese of Logandale, Nevada, says she tries to support her husband in his church work because "I know that our marriage is strengthened when he magnifies his priesthood and his callings." But giving support goes both ways. Faye Sowards says she bets her husband "is one of the few men who's ever taught charm and poise to a Merrie Miss class—I was too sick to go and couldn't get a substitute."

When Sherry Bratsman of Sugar City, Idaho, was called to be ward Relief Society president, she hesitated because of her several young children. But "my husband assured me I could do the job and that he would help in any way." He had a chance to make good on that promise a few months ago when one of the babies was quite sick the same day Sherry had arranged to interview thirty visiting teachers. "I was ready to call them all and arrange for a different time, but my husband took the morning off and stayed with the children so I could fill my responsibility."

A Lot of Thoughtfulness

Many other ways of expressing love came up frequently: thinking the best of one another; being proud of each other and showing it; complimenting instead of criticizing; following the golden rule; solving problems in reasonable, calm, relaxed ways; listening to, understanding, and valuing each other's ideas, for example. Another extremely popular way of demonstrating love is to do simple things for each other—planned or unplanned, expected or unexpected, sincere, heartfelt, thoughtful, and personal.

The letters provided many more ideas than can be listed, contributed by many more people than can be named. But here's a sample:

He takes his shoes off (for the first day at least) when she washes the kitchen floor. She hides chocolate mints or gum for him in his drawer. He does all the cooking on their camping trips so she can have a vacation, too. She records *Ensign* and *Church News* articles, personal messages, and songs and greetings from the kids for him to listen to during his long road trips. He gives her a steering wheel knob with a flower embedded inside, saying, "Here's a rose that won't make you sneeze." She gives him a five-pound box of homemade cookies with a note promising to keep the cookie jar filled for an entire year. He surprises her with a delicious birthday breakfast, complete with her brothers and sisters and their spouses. ("There was only one problem," she says: "the guest of honor looked like she just got out of bed!") He comes home from work very tired and finds the table beautifully set for a candlelight dinner for two. She smiles and tells him he's the best-looking man in the ward. He responds, "Just in the ward?"

Not all expressions of love need to be spontaneous, though. Some couples like to come up with and faithfully maintain traditions. For example, Don Center of Topeka, Kansas, says he and his wife exchange "I love you" gifts on the first day of every month; the gifts have to be different every time, and they can't cost any money. But Jane Willie and her husband, newlyweds living in Salt Lake City, can't wait for the first of each month. They celebrate every Thursday (the day they got married) with a special dinner, gifts, and time together to review their courtship and strengthen their love.

Celebrating "all-time firsts" is another idea. "It helps show love and occasionally prevents hurt feelings," says Mary Seely of Brigham City, Utah. Early in their marriage, a broken glass was one of their "all-time firsts." Just the other day, they celebrated another "first": the last glass of that set was broken.

Time together is an essential tradition, and according to the letters we received, available time really isn't that hard to find if you try. Wanting a few quiet moments alone with her husband daily, Patricia Peterson of Camarillo, California, gets up with him at 5:15 every morning, prepares him a good breakfast which they enjoy together, and packs him a lunch. Several couples hire a babysitter on a permanent Friday night basis so there's no weekly hassle trying to find one.

Elder Stuart Knell and his wife, Winifred, serving together

in the Bristol England Mission, have found, after forty years of married life, "the perfect answer to happy marriage"—in the missionary handbook, of all places. There they are encouraged, like all missionaries, to take the time weekly to hold companionship evaluation sessions. Doing this, they say, "we love and understand each other more, and we have talked together more in the last four months than all of our married life. We even discuss the things which irritate us, and we are both in our middle sixties."

Some couples get away alone for an overnight vacation at least once a year, feeling that babysitter wages are a good investment in their marriage. Long bus rides to stake temple excursions provide an ideal time to be together and talk. And some wives frequently accompany their husbands on out-of-town business trips just for a chance to be alone together.

Other traditions involve flowers. Mrs. Leon Searle of Midvale, Utah, remembers the love both of her parents had for roses and how painstakingly they cared for their rose garden. "Dad would always pick the first rose that bloomed in the summer," she says, "and present it to my mother with a kiss. He continued to do this every morning until the last rose faded in the fall." And Judy S. Russell of Mesa, Arizona, loves her husband's flower-giving tradition because it's so untraditional: "I never get flowers for Mother's Day, our anniversary, or any other special occasion," she says. "But I do get them when the weather is bad, or I am sick, or just because the sun shines—and I know I am loved."

Like many of the Saints who wrote, Mervyn Dykes of Wellington, New Zealand, found it impossible to explain all the things his wife does to show her love. But an important reason he loves her, he says, is that she loves him—even though neither he nor their life together is exactly what she dreamed of when she was a schoolgirl. She thought she'd marry someone small-boned and slender with dark, flashing eyes. But she got a blond, green-eyed, 230-pound discus thrower. She loves to collect dainty furniture, but has four overly energetic children and a husband who demolishes chairs just by sitting on them. She used to sing for large audiences in concert halls, but is now usually accompanied only by the drier in the laundry. Yet, she's content with her husband and her life.

"One day not so long ago," Mervyn tells, "she walked up to me, all smiles, and firmly pressed a thick slice of bread and jam into my face."

" 'Why did you do that?' I spluttered.

" 'Because I've always wanted to do it to someone,' she grinned. 'And there wasn't a custard cream pie handy.'

"Then she giggled and sped out of the room, pursued by a large discus thrower threateningly waving the remains of a slice of bread and jam.

"Really," he concludes, "is it any wonder I love her?"

Marvin K. Gardner, member of the General Music Committee of the Church and assistant managing editor of the Ensign, *resides in the Bountiful Sixteenth Ward and is the father of four children.*

CHASTITY IN MARRIAGE

Sacred Power, Used with Wisdom

In the process of learning what is right for you, it is helpful to use this basic measuring stick: Is it selfish?

By Dr. Homer Ellsworth

As a gynecologist, I am frequently asked questions concerning family planning from active and committed Latter-day Saint women who wonder about the Church's stand on this issue. Here are some of the principles and attitudes I believe apply to these fundamental questions that most couples ask themselves many times during their child-bearing years.

I rejoice in our basic understanding of the plan of salvation, which teaches us that we come to earth for growth and maturity, and for testing. In that process we may marry and provide temporal bodies for our Heavenly Father's spirit children. That's basic, it seems to me. In contemplating this truth, I also take great delight in the Church's affirmative position that it is our blessing and joy, and our spiritual obligation, to bear children and to have a family. It impresses me that the positive is stressed as our goal.

I rejoice in our understanding that one of the most fundamental principles in the plan of salvation is free agency. The opportunity to make choices is so important that our Heavenly Father was willing to withhold additional opportunities from a third of his children rather than deprive them of their right of choice. This principle of free agency is vital to the success of our probation. Many of the decisions we make involve the application of principles where precise yes-and-no answers are just not available in Church handbooks, meetings, or even the scriptures.

Our growth process, then, results from weighing the alternatives, studying the matter carefully, and seeking inspiration from the Lord. This, it seems to me, is at the heart of the gospel plan. It has always given me great joy and confidence to observe that in their administration of God's teachings, our inspired prophets do not seek to violate this general plan of individual agency, but operate within broad guidelines that provide considerable individual flexibility.

I recall a President of the Church, now deceased, who visited his daughter in the hospital following a miscarriage. She was the mother of eight children and was in her early forties. She asked, "Father, may I quit now?" His response was, "Don't ask me. That decision is between you, your husband, and your Father in Heaven. If you two can face him with a good conscience and can say you have done the best you could, that you have really tried, then you may quit. But, that is between you and him. I have enough problems of my own to talk over with him when we meet!" So it is clear to me that the decisions regarding our children, when to have them, their number, and all related matters and questions can only be made after real discussion between the marriage partners and after prayer.

In this process of learning what is right for you at any particular time, I have always found it helpful to use a basic measuring stick: *Is it selfish?* I have concluded that most of our sins are really sins of selfishness. If you don't pay your tithing, selfishness is at the heart of it. If you commit adultery, selfishness is at the heart of it. If you are dishonest, selfishness is at the heart of it. I have noted that many times in the scriptures we observe the Lord chastising people because of their selfishness. Thus, on the family questions, if we limit our families because we are self-centered or materialistic, we will surely develop a character based on selfishness. As the scriptures make clear, that is not a description of a celestial character. I have found that we really have to analyze ourselves to discover which of our motives are superficial.

But, on the other hand, we need not be afraid of studying the question from important angles—the physical or mental health of the mother and father, the parents' capacity to provide basic necessities, and so on. If for certain personal reasons a couple prayerfully decides that having another child immediately is unwise, the method of spacing children—discounting possible medical or physical effects—makes little difference. Abstinence, of course, is also a form of contraception, and like any other method it has side effects, some of which are harmful to the marriage relationship.

As a physician I am often required to treat social-emotional symptoms related to various aspects of living. In doing so I have always been impressed that our prophets past and present have never stipulated that bearing children was the sole function of the marriage relationship. Prophets have taught that physical intimacy is a strong force in strengthening the love bond in marriage, enhancing and reinforcing marital unity. Indeed, it is the rightful gift of God to the married. As the Apostle Paul says, "The wife hath not power of her own body, but the husband; and likewise also the husband hath not power of his own body, but the wife." Paul continues, "Depart ye not one from the other, except it be with consent for a time, that ye may give yourselves to fasting and prayer; and come together again, that Satan tempt you not for your incontinency." (1 Corinthians 7:4-5, Joseph Smith Translation). Abstinence in marriage, Paul says, can cause unnecessary temptations and tensions, which are certainly harmful side effects.

So, as to the number and spacing of children, and other related questions on this subject, such decisions are to be made by husband and wife righteously and empathetically communicating together and seeking the inspiration of the Lord. I believe that the prophets have given wise counsel when they advise couples to be considerate and plan carefully so that the mother's health will not be impaired. When this recommendation of the First Presidency is ignored or unknown or misinterpreted, heartache can result.

I know a couple who had seven children. The wife, who was afflicted with high blood pressure, had been advised by her physician that additional pregnancy was fraught with grave danger and should not be attempted. But the couple interpreted the teachings of their local priesthood leaders to mean that they should consider no contraceptive measures under any circumstances. She died from a stroke during the delivery of her eighth child.

As I meet other people and learn of their circumstances, I am continually inspired by the counsel of the First Presidency in the *General Handbook of Instructions* that the health of the mother and the well-being of the family should be considered. Thirty-four years as a practicing gynecologist and as an observer of Latter-day Saint families have taught me that not only the physical well-being but the emotional well-being must also be considered. Some parents are less subject to mood swings and depression and can more easily cope with the pressures of many children. Some parents have more help from their families and friends. Some are more effective parents than others, even when their desire and motivation are the same. In addition, parents do owe their children the necessities of life. The desire for luxuries, of course, would not be an appropriate determinant of family size; luxuries are not a legitimate consideration. I think every inspired human heart can quickly determine what is a luxury and what is not.

In summary, it is clear to me that couples should not let the things that matter most be at the mercy of those that matter least. In searching for what is most important, I believe that we are accountable not only for what we do, but for why we do it. Thus, regarding family size, spacing of children, and attendant questions, we should desire to multiply and replenish the earth as the Lord commands us. In that process, Heavenly Father intends that we use the free agency he has given in charting a wise course for ourselves and our families. We gain the wisdom to chart that wise course through study, prayer, and listening to the still small voice within us.

Homer Ellsworth, physician-surgeon-M.D., is the father of nine children and serves as a counselor in the Salt Lake Temple presidency.

Keeping the Marriage Covenant

They thought their marriage was too strong to be threatened.

An active LDS couple recently lived through a situation they thought they'd never experience: infidelity—or, in their case, a dangerous brush with it. The impact on their lives was severe, but the gospel of Jesus Christ has enabled them to experience the fruits of repentance and forgiveness and to strengthen their characters. They are indeed wiser now—and from their painful lesson, they have realized the truth of certain principles. The principles aren't new; they have heard them many times before. But now they have a personal testimony of them—and a strong desire to help others avoid the tragedy.

1. *Don't ever think you're immune.* A year ago, both Jim and Susan (their names have been changed) would have ridiculed the idea that either of them could ever become involved with anyone else. Theirs was a good marriage—they were living happily in a relationship that had begun with a temple wedding. But because they had grown secure with each other, they felt safe from worldly temptations; they didn't fully comprehend the power Satan has to prey on personal weaknesses, or the human tendency to rationalize when powerful emotions are involved. They were simply too naive to recognize a potentially dangerous situation.

2. *Constantly keep up your spiritual reserves.* Jim and Susan now feel that if they had made a more conscious effort to pray and study the scriptures daily, individually and as a family, they would have felt more clearly the influence of the Spirit of the Lord in their lives. The Spirit can more than alert us to possible dangers; it can also keep husbands and wifes working together, united as one.

3. *Use idle time wisely.* Last winter, for the first time in their marriage, Jim's work schedule was such that he was home alone in the afternoons. All of the children were finally in school, and Susan had gotten a job. Unused to being home by himself, Jim became lonely and restless. It certainly would have been healthier and much safer if he had decided to use his free time on some demanding project or activity—but he chose instead to frequently visit with friends, simply killing time.

4. *Recognize potential dangers in one-to-one visiting.* The Church has long cautioned its members to go home teaching or visiting teaching in pairs, and to avoid one-man/one-woman situations—even things like driving to Church meetings together. In the past, Jim and Susan scoffed at that, considering the advice excessive. But now they no longer consider the precaution overstated.

Because Jim had so many free afternoons and so few specific plans, he began dropping in on Susan's best friend, Liz (a fictitious name also). At first this visiting was quite innocent. The two families had been good friends for a long time, and both spouses knew of the visits. Besides, since there were always several small children present, the two of them felt they weren't really alone together. The little children, however, weren't adequate chaperones.

Unfortunately, Liz and her husband weren't communicating well with each other at the time, and she felt she needed some emotional support. Because of Jim's visits, she gradually began to rely on him for some of that support. He, in turn, recognized her need to talk out problems, and sometimes felt much like a counselor as he talked with her. Gradually, however, Jim found himself in conversations with Liz that he would have been embarrassed to repeat—intimate topics and details of private matters. The attraction of such discussion was strong—and Jim now sees how he rationalized his actions.

5. *Maintain open communication between husband and wife.* Jim and Susan had always been able to talk about anything. Yet, it should have served as a flashing warning signal when he stopped sharing the specifics of his visits. The proper sense of formality and reserve had disappeared between him and Liz. Sadly, Jim did not feel unfaithful to Susan, but truthfully he was already beginning to redirect his interests, although he didn't want to admit it or face up to it.

6. *Satan can subtly lead us toward sin in such small steps that we may not even recognize what is happening.* What had started as a normal friendship between two married people began to get completely out of hand, and even now it is difficult and embarrassing for them to face up to what happened. Liz gradually became too emotionally dependent on Jim, and he didn't know how to back away without hurting her—nor did he really want to—for there was an attraction developing that motivated Jim more than he wanted to admit. Little by little the emotional need was permitted to devolve into a physical interest. The descent was so gradual that each step seemed not to be much more compromising than the last. The process happened so insidiously and compellingly that they ignored the laws that should have been governing their lives.

7. *It's hard to simply back out of a sinful situation.* Finally, however, they realized that boundaries had been passed that shouldn't have been. Jim didn't want to tell Susan what was happening because he was ashamed, afraid of hurting her and of losing her respect. He also knew she valued Liz's friendship highly, and he could see that this would injure that relationship. Largely, though, as a result of the increasing attraction, Jim didn't want to stop seeing Liz, and he rationalized that her dependence on him was too delicate a thing for him to abandon completely. So he convinced himself that he could reverse the flow of events and simply back the situation up to proper levels again. But his rationalization didn't work. Each time they were together, even though he rationalized that he could control things, they became more involved instead of less.

At this point, even greater tragedy could have occurred. Fortunately, however, the story has a better ending than it might have had. Guilt pressed on Jim, and thoroughly aghast at his condition, he faced up to himself, his wife, and his children.

He felt a deep sense of sorrow and regret for what he had pulled Liz and her husband—his good friend—into. He realized that he had placed himself at the edge of spiritual and marital peril and in the process was bringing ruin to his family and everything that had meant the most to him. He therefore bought and read President Spencer W. Kimball's book, *The Miracle of Forgiveness* and realized that if he were going to free himself, he would need to do it the Lord's way—through confession and complete change.

With terrible wrenching, he went both to Susan and to his bishop. He says that, of the two, it was much harder approaching Susan because he knew she would be overwhelmed with despair and confusion. And she was. The first few days after he talked to her, they both felt as if the world were crumbling apart. But, together, they have coped. Both did a great deal of weeping those first weeks as they tried to make sense of the situation and reach out to each other again. In the process, they learned as much about recovery from sin as about the entry into it.

The bishop was sensitive and supportive—and Jim and Susan are both very grateful for his spiritual counsel. He knew how sincere Jim's sorrow was and helped him have hope in his ability to get his life in order and obtain forgiveness. He also talked with Susan, letting her just talk out her feelings. At the same time, the bishop was firm in his counsel, pointing out that Jim's involvement with Liz must come to an immediate and complete halt, whatever it took—even if it meant moving away to remove himself from the source of temptation.

In the Lord's own way, and after the passage of time, Jim was able to know forgiveness and peace again. "I have understood the meaning of a 'broken heart and a contrite spirit' in a more real sense than ever before," Jim says. "We've both been scoured internally, but our hearts have been touched and healed. Because we want to have a stronger relationship with each other and be obedient to the Lord's commandments, we've tried to put our family's spiritual affairs more in order. We now start each day kneeling in prayer, and we study the scriptures as a family every evening. We think we are more teachable now. We know we have to rely on the safeguards of the gospel."

Susan's recovery was understandably difficult. "I know I have been touched by the Spirit," she says, "and I've received undeniable confirmation of my husband's love and his ability to be strong and stable in the future. Although I have had frequent periods of extreme depression, there has been a tangible force for healing in my life. I try not to think of the past, but instead let the memories gradually dissolve from my mind."

But there was still the matter of resolving their relationship with the other family. Both couples attended the same ward and would be in weekly contact. "Forgiving my husband was, in fact, the easier task for me," says Susan. "But how should we act toward the other couple?" In trying to work through her feelings, Susan was blessed with some insights new to her. "To be honest," she admits, "my earliest reaction toward my old friend was hostile. But one night I suddenly understood during an anguished prayer that I had to release my hatred and be forgiving before I could be free of the chains that were holding *me* bound. Like Jim, I too began to feel sorrow for the tragedy that had been brought into our friends' lives."

The couples are now on speaking terms with each other. Jim has come to the solid understanding that there must always be a distinct emotional distance between himself and any person of the opposite sex, and that a breach in proper relationships must never happen again. He is now convinced that there is great security, after all, in the kind of healthy caution we are all counseled to maintain.

Jim and Susan have spent a lot of time lately reconfirming and strengthening their marriage bonds. "It was a sad experience," Jim says, "but we're determined to learn from it." Susan's temporary job ended, and she was again able to be home full time. That, in itself, has been beneficial, since, they admit, the stresses put on them by her continued absences were a significant factor in the original trouble. "We spend afternoons together," Susan says, "doing things we particularly enjoy—swimming, bowling, hiking,—and we have started some house projects together. We have especially spent a lot of time just talking and simply being close to each other."

Jim and Susan's experience may seem unlikely and contrived. But it happened. "Because of our experience,"

Susan says, "we're more aware than ever that we shouldn't be so naive as to think we are immune to temptation. Now we're trying harder than ever to protect ourselves and our family by keeping the Spirit alive in our home and by really obeying the counsel of our leaders. As a result we feel confident that we will be both a cautious and a more securely happy couple."

Chastity: A Principle of Power

This positive principle helps us to understand ourselves, acquire spiritual power, build enduring relationships, and grow closer to God.

By Steve Gilliland

Those of us who work with young people know it's not unusual to hear the following comment: "All I ever hear about sex from parents and teachers is that it's sinful. Isn't there something positive to be said about chastity?" Latter-day Saints can reply that there most certainly is! The gospel gives us a clear and wholesome perspective on chastity. That is especially obvious when gospel teachings are contrasted with teachings of the secular world.

For instance, the religions of man have taught that the physical body is evil and that the spirit must struggle to overcome it and be liberated from it. But the restored gospel says quite the opposite: the body is a blessing. We came to earth to obtain a body and to make it a part of us as a means for further progress. Without it we cannot receive a fullness of joy (see D&C 93:33-35). Without it we will not be liberated, but will be in bondage (see Joseph F. Smith—Vision 1:50). The gospel teaches that we are exalted *with* our bodies, not in spite of them.

Paul seemed to be suggesting the same thing when he said, "He that committeth fornication sinneth *against* his own body." (1 Corinthians 6:18; italics added.)

A second false teaching is that the intimate experiences of

marriage are a necessary evil. Yet such experiences when enjoyed in accord with God's commandments and the Spirit can enrich one's life and enliven the soul. President Kimball has referred to conjugal relationships in marriage as "inherently good." (*Ensign*, Oct. 1975, p. 4; see also *Journal of Discourses*, 26:217.) "Sex can be a wonderful servant but a terrible master; it can be a creative force more powerful than any other in the fostering of love, companionship, happiness." (Spencer W. Kimball quoting Billy Graham, *Ensign*, May 1974, p. 8.)

A third false teaching is that man is basically evil simply *because* of his physical nature. The scriptures, however, do not support this. They teach that people become "carnal, sensual, and devilish" *only* as they begin to follow Satan (see Moses 5:13 and D&C 20:20).

King Benjamin makes this clear. "Man is an enemy to God," he said, "*unless* he yields to the enticings of the Holy Spirit." (Mosiah 3:19, italics added.)

The truth is that chastity is a godly virtue, and "the natural man receiveth not the things of the Spirit of God: they are foolishness unto him: neither can he know them, because they are spiritually discerned." (1 Corinthians 2:14.) Consequently, only those who are spiritual can understand spiritual things. Thus, the world will never fully understand why we live the law of chastity. But Latter-day Saints *can* understand and appreciate it.

Builds Personal Strength and Understanding

President David O. McKay said that a necessary ingredient of spirituality is "a consciousness of victory over self" (*Improvement Era*, Dec. 1969, p. 31). Two great blessings that can come from chastity are self-mastery and self-knowledge.

The *letter* of the law of chastity is to have sexual experiences only with one's spouse, the man or woman with whom legal marriage covenants have been made. But the spirit of this law encompasses far more. It requires that we keep sacred and appropriate all of our sexual desires—and all related behaviors. To have physical desires is not evil. But to dwell upon them *is* evil. This is lust—the mental pursuit of anything that would be spiritually damaging.

Lust causes one to draw his attention away from that which is spiritually productive and fulfilling—to focus upon nonfulfilling and spiritually damaging thoughts and actions. It is a mental narcotic that draws us away from our long-range goals. It can lead us to sacrifice all that is valuable for a momentary experience and leaves us with nothing but pain and sorrow and confusion.

But what if a person, because of previous conditioning, has immoral desires? The same principle applies: the presence of desire is not an indication of sin. The issue is, what does one do with the desire? Is it used to inflame, or is it recognized and then forthrightly directed to take its place offstage with other feelings and thoughts that one does not wish to dwell upon? President Kimball has informed us that even individuals tempted with homosexual or other abnormal tendencies can—with patience, commitment, and faith—control such desires and permit normal desires to awaken and take precedence over the abnormal.[1] As a counselor and a bishop, I have seen this happen in a number of lives.

A conscious effort to develop self-mastery can help us to understand ourselves. As I define my behavior, I see more clearly the kind of person I am right now. The degree to which I keep my chastity covenant also generally reflects how strong or weak I am in other areas of my life, and indicates to me how committed to celestial ideals I really am. On the other hand, instead of confronting and working out confusing feelings such as loneliness or inadequacy, Satan would have a person try to flee from them through immorality. But such escapes are only temporary, and so the person seeks to flee again and again, forever unsuccessfully. As a result, Satan leads one into further confusion through unchastity.

Chastity requires discipline. In developing discipline in my own life I have become aware of my uniqueness. I've discovered that I need to avoid certain kinds of movies, certain literature, certain situations, and so on. Although others claim they cause them no problems, they may cause problems for me. When I've rationalized that since others can do those things with no apparent harm, I should be able to also, I've ended up with more thoughts to control, more mental images to suppress. I wanted to control a fire, and found I was adding more fuel. This more complete appreciation of chastity has required me to understand and work with my own personal spiritual chemistry. I have to decide, with the help of the Spirit, where I must draw the line.

The most valuable kind of self-knowledge is not just stored in our minds, but is felt deep within our souls through confronting the many stimuli that the media and life bombard us with. This self-knowledge requires continued faith and commitment in the face of setbacks, strength that comes from pulling ourselves free from the tentacles of temptation. It feels good to be in control! In an important sense, then, chastity is the disciplining of our sexual desires and behaviors and the gaining of full understanding and control of self in all areas related to sexuality.

Builds Enduring Relationships

Chastity is also a great force in building the quality of our personal relationships. During the important courtship period, chaste couples spend their time working on understanding and communicating and wisely assessing their thoughts about each other, instead of fleeing reality by indulging in improper intimacies. Chastity frees the couple to work on building a potentially eternal companionship.[2] It brings a proper perspective to a very compelling power. The world makes sex all-important; chastity helps us to see it as one of many important facets of marriage. The world also tells us that our primary concern with desire should be personal gratification. This can lead to a relationship based upon selfishness. The emphasis is on getting, not giving. But chastity places spiritual needs above gratification; it places the emphasis on giving, not on getting. It requires personal restraint out of love for one's companion. Alma counseled his son to "bridle all your passions, that ye may be filled with love." (Alma 38:12.)

President Kimball has explained that the sexual experience has two purposes: bringing children into the world and expressing "that kind of love between a man and wife that makes for true oneness." (*Ensign*, May 1974, p.7.) He has also said that "we know of no directive from the Lord that proper sexual experience between husbands and wives need be limited totally to the procreation of children, but we find much evidence from Adam until now that no provision was ever made by the Lord for indiscriminate sex." (*Ensign*, Oct. 1975, p.4.)

These two purposes give us guidelines about how we can keep these powers sacred and holy and within the bounds the Lord has established. Within marriage an attitude that totally ignores the needs and sensitivities of one's spouse would violate this sacred purpose. Also, solitary tampering with these powers perverts this sacred design. It can condition one to focus on one's own needs, inflame lust, and shrink the capacity to overcome.[3] It focuses again on getting rather than giving. It should be clear that a couple who is chaste before marriage probably has developed sound attitudes for this relationship after marriage.

The chaste couple is concerned about strengthening each other. Their feelings of responsibility prevent them from doing anything that would weaken or tempt each other. Modesty in speech and dress are as much for the protection of others and one's partner, as for one's self.

This concern goes far beyond the physical relationship. When a person is chaste and true in all ways, he becomes part of an ever stronger, ever richer relationship. Chastity not only demonstrates love for one's companion, but also for one's children, who can be born under temple covenants and enjoy wholesome examples in an eternal family.

Builds Richer Relationships with God

President McKay said that "the pathway to God leads through the heart of man." Our communion with God is powerfully affected by our relations with others. And conversely, our relations with others require divine guidance in order to become mature and eternal. Love is the most divine attribute we can develop. But if we pursue acts of selfishness we make it difficult for the Holy Ghost to attend us. As we deny his influence, our relationship with God deteriorates, and feelings of insecurity, irritation, and self-centeredness arise. Then, because we lack one of the great sustaining, positive forces in our lives—the Spirit of the Lord—we become trapped in our doubts and fears, we make demands for reassurance that our partners are incapable of meeting, and through the whole process we become insensitive to the needs of those around us, including our partner. Nothing can destroy a relationship faster than this kind of atmosphere.

Chastity, on the other hand, permits the Holy Ghost to influence us, and enhances trust, which is the basis for any enduring relationship. Through our love for others, we can recognize and understand our love for our Heavenly Father and his Son, Jesus Christ. And this is the most important relationship of all (see D&C 132:21).

To fully give ourselves to the Lord, we must first have control of ourselves. Discipleship requires discipline. Before one is ready to live the law of consecration, wherein he gives his all to the Lord, he must live the law of chastity; to live the law of chastity, he must apply the laws of sacrifice and obedience. As one does this, his confidence will "wax strong in the presence of God" (D&C 121:45), and he will "receive the pleasing word of God, and feast upon his love" (Jacob 3:2). The joy, the peace, and the power that this generates are hard to describe. Of this experience President McKay said, "To feel one's faculties unfolding and truth expanding in the soul is one of life's sublimest experiences." (*Improvement Era* Dec. 1969, p. 31.)

We can never fully know and love God unless we live the kind of life he lives. When I was younger, I was sometimes critical of some Church leaders and the decisions they made. Since then I have been a bishop, and now I see things in a very different perspective. I am less tempted to criticize, because I am more aware of the problems and feelings of a bishop. In the same way, as we become godlike, we begin to understand God better. Our relationship with him becomes richer. Mosiah tells us that as we serve the Lord we will come closer to "the thoughts and intents of his heart." (Mosiah 5:13.) When we live as he lives, we learn to care as he cares and feel as he feels. Chastity, as much as any other gospel principle, helps us to know him because it promotes essential godly qualities such as understanding, self-mastery, love, and compassion.

When I become tired in my struggles against temptation, I recall that Jesus "was in all points tempted like as we are, yet without sin." (Hebrews 4:15.) He was blessed with a physical body which he learned to master. Like us, he had the capacity for spiritual fatigue (see D&C 19:18). Certainly Satan tried in every way to make him sin. So, no matter how hard it is for me, I know that Jesus climbed a similar path many years ago. Because he understands fully our mortal condition, he is able to help and strengthen us along the way. We can be eternally grateful that when we confess and forsake our sins he will remember them no more (see D&C 58:42-43). Throughout the eternities they cannot have a hold upon us because of the Savior's atoning sacrifice. What a joy to know that you and I can become clean—totally clean—from our own sins!

As we see the vital role sexuality plays in our total mortal development, we can gain some understanding of why the Lord, in his love for us, gave us the law of chastity. "How glorious is he who lives the chaste life. He walks unfearful. . . . He is honored and respected. . . . He is loved by the Lord, for he stands without blemish. The exaltations of eternities await his coming."[4]

Steve Gilliland, director of the Institute of Religion, California State University at Long Beach, and father of eight children, serves as Scoutmaster of the Lakewood, California, First Ward.

Notes:
1. Spencer W. Kimball, *A Letter to a Friend* (Salt Lake City, Utah: The Church of Jesus Christ of Latter-day Saints, 1978).
2. Steve Gilliland, "The Psychological Case for Chastity," *Ensign*, July 1975, pp. 54-58.
3. Boyd K. Packer, *To Young Men Only* (Salt Lake City: The Church of Jesus Christ of Latter-day Saints, 1976), pp. 4-5.
4. First Presidency statement issued 3 Oct. 1942. Quoted in J.R. Clark, *Messages of the First Presidency* (Salt Lake City: Bookcraft, 1975), pp. 174-77.

SHARING FEELINGS

Keeping in Touch with Feelings

It's one of the most important things in a marriage. Yet many husbands and wives are emotionally tongue-tied.

By C. Richard Chidester

I'd always thought I grew up in a family where a lot of sharing went on and where feelings were out in the open. Then, in graduate school, I married and I discovered that in all too many ways I still fit into the stereotype of the American male. I wanted to come across as aggressive, objective, and rational. Showing feelings openly, I thought, would be a sign of weakness or lack of control. Yet there was plenty to make me feel unsure in the adjustments to marriage and to graduate school. As the pressures mounted, I did the worst possible thing. I clammed up.

I didn't realize that silence communicates too; my wife, going through her own adjustments, became very uncomfortable and anxious because she didn't know what was causing my feelings. She could only wonder: Did I hate her cooking? Was school getting me down? Was I homesick for my own family? Did I regret marrying her? She also wondered why she was so powerless to do anything about my feelings. She was happy; things were going well for her. But what was wrong with me? Why wasn't I happy?

We were both pretty tense by the time I finally got up the

courage to tell her what the pressures of school were doing to me. Then I discovered she was so receptive it was easy for me to talk to her. When I realized how she'd been feeling, I was overwhelmed. I told her how happy I was with her and our marriage and asked her not to take my moods personally when I was feeling anxious or discouraged. Once she realized what was going on inside me, she understood. And both of us realized that the best thing she could do was just listen. I needed to feel supported in dealing with my own feelings, but she no longer felt that she had to take responsibility for changing my negative feelings into positive ones.

In some ways, that moment of true understanding was the beginning of our marriage—of being so close that we are truly one. Closeness comes on a continuum. We have "superficial" encounters with a clerk or service station attendant; we have "casual" relationships with a neighbor or someone who works in our building; we have a "close" relationship with a bishop, a friend, a trusted colleague; we move into "involved" relationships when we are consistently sharing feelings honestly within our families or with close friends. But "intimacy," a most profound and tender kind of closeness, is comparatively rare. In intimate relationships, we share feelings we normally keep hidden—doubts and fears, joys and sorrows, hopes and dreams. Most people marry out of a hunger for intimacy, but few achieve it. In fact, I feel that a great deal of suffering and loneliness in relationships can be traced back to a lack of intimacy.

Intimacy, then, means sharing feelings. My emotions are the key to *me*. Behind my behavior lies my emotions; how I feel about things shapes my actions in the future. Since I interpret my experience on an emotional level, being in touch with my feelings provides my most important information about my real self. My emotional reactions tell me about my needs, my self-image, my values, my sensitivities, my fears, and my strengths. If I can recognize my feelings and ask "Why did that comment make me anxious?" or "Why does playing with my children make me feel so good?" then I am learning to know myself on a profound level. If I can share these emotions with others, I am sharing myself. And the rewards—in feeling understood and accepted—are powerful. Another reward is in freedom; covering up emotions literally drains physical energy and causes tension.

Elder Marvin J. Ashton, commenting on the importance of communication in families, pointed out that "communication is more than a sharing of words. It is the wise sharing of emotions, feelings, and concerns. It is the sharing of oneself totally." (*Ensign*, May 1976, p. 52.)

If sharing feelings is so important, why don't people do it more often?—especially when all of us yearn for that kind of closeness. I remember one woman saying wistfully, "We've been married twenty-two years and I'd really like to know my husband. But he'll never tell me how he's feeling." She is not the only one I've heard that comment from.

One reason that wistful plea has remained unanswered for twenty-two years is that intimacy also carries with it a terrifying risk. Since sharing feelings reveals so much about us, we become vulnerable. What if we are misunderstood or rejected if we share feelings? This is a real fear, and sometimes it is justified. I know a woman who wanted to be closer to her husband, so she shared with him how hurt she felt when he was sarcastic about her in public. After this revelation, whenever this immature husband wanted to hurt her out of spite, he would purposely make fun of her when others were present. The toll on relationships and self-esteem in such a situation is a heavy one.

Another reason we hesitate to share our feelings comes from the expectations we pick up from others. No one is more emotionally honest than a baby; but as that baby grows up, he learns that "big boys don't cry" and she learns that "you aren't pretty when you pout." Parents must teach their children to control their emotions, but instead they all too frequently teach them to repress their emotions. The delicate balance is to learn how to acknowledge emotions and to express them appropriately.

That was the situation my wife and I were in when we realized what my cover-up was doing to our own relationship. We'd both learned pretty clearly what society expected from us, and it has taken serious attention to keep us feeling close. Please believe me; it's worth it. I know it's worth it for our marriage, and other couples that I've worked with have expressed the same feelings: "We talked about things we'd never told each other before." "I felt more warmth and love for my wife than I've felt for years."

Here are some suggestions on how to deal with our feelings and share them more effectively:

1. Accept the concept that feelings are honorable. We don't need to feel guilty about having feelings.

2. Learn to identify them properly and express them appropriately. We need to let our rational selves mediate so that we aren't unleashing our emotions in an immature way. Thinking also helps us identify which emotions we should share openly in a healthy way and which ones we should handle privately.

3. Express emotions by describing them. For example: "Right now I'm feeling frustrated about my problems at work" or "I feel so discouraged about the way the children have been acting lately; I would really like to talk to you about it" or "I feel so much more relaxed about the way I'm handling my Sunday School class now." If you haven't been used to doing this, it might be helpful to follow a simple model: When __________ happens, I feel __________ because __________. For example, if a husband neglects to call his wife when he is going to be late getting home, his wife will probably be upset. She could focus those feelings of anger outwards: "You're the most inconsiderate person I know! The least you could do is call!" Or she could describe her feelings: "When you don't call if you're going to be late, I feel anxious and frightened because I'm worried something may have happened to you."

4. Treat negative feelings respectfully, not guiltily. I've always been impressed with how open the Savior was about his negative feelings. In only one example, in 3 Nephi, we read that he is "troubled" because of Israel's wickedness; but just a few verses later, he is saying, "My joy is full" because of the faithfulness of the people. (3 Nephi 17:14, 20.)

Many people feel that negative feelings are wrong, so they try to act as if they feel something else. The result is a double message, for it is simply impossible to express spontaneous love—or any other kind of positive emotion—under those circumstances. If the family rules allow the open and respectful expression of negative feelings ("*When* you did that, I *felt* hurt *because* . . ."), then positive feelings would flow more freely too.

Another temptation when you have negative feelings is to "let it all hang out." Usually, this philosophy is actually a license to hurt. When the Apostle Paul told us to "speak . . . the truth in love" (Ephesians 4:15), I think he was telling us that we must share negative feelings in sensitive, non-threatening ways, being honest but in a way that will not make others feel defensive or put down. Sharing feelings is not an excuse to punish, blame, or insult.

5. Don't criticize the other person's feelings or try to change them. Only the person who has the feelings can change them. We can help most by listening and empathizing, but we may only make our mates feel worse if we say, "You shouldn't feel that way," or "I can't imagine why you feel that way." They may decide to stop talking to us since we only make them feel worse.

We can show empathy by supportive listening—eye contact, nods, pats, or hugs. We can also reflect our mate's feelings by saying things such as, "It sounds as if you're really worn out" or "You seem really happy with the way things have turned out." Receiving our mate's self-revelations without judgments, criticism, or rejection is so important that I wish I could think of a stronger way to say it. I think the main reason so many couples never achieve intimacy is that they can't create a climate for real sharing by being warm and understanding when they listen. Too many of us react defensively when we hear our mate express feelings.

6. Keep in touch. Sharing feelings isn't just for marathon sessions or crisis times. My wife and I have found it useful to get in touch with each other's feelings each morning by asking, "How are you feeling?" or "How are you doing?" or by saying, "Today I'm feeling . . . ." It only takes a few moments but we know where the other person stands, physically, emotionally, spiritually, and in other ways. We have a sense of oneness and really feel motivated to be supportive and understanding. On days when we've neglected this "getting in touch," I can tell the difference in just one day; and frequently the difference shows up in how effectively we relate with each other and with our children. It's so important to keep in touch that if I leave

before she wakes up in the morning, we touch base on the phone during the day.

What differences does it make to have this kind of intimacy in a home? Let me tell you what difference it makes to us. As I hold monthly interviews with my children to set goals and instruct them, the highlight for me comes when we get down to how they're feeling about themselves, the family, school, church, the way we're treating them, etc. When feelings of anxiety and inferiority surface, I can get at the roots of the problems, not just the symptoms. Hearing and understanding our children's feelings makes them feel loved. It helps us as parents adjust our behavior to deal with them more effectively. Most important, these interviews give me an open invitation to share my positive feelings about my children.

I'll never forget the thrill I felt one night after the children had watched *Heidi* on television. The members of that family had talked about their love for each other and had demonstrated it in ways that moved our children. We talked about it while I helped get the children ready for bed; and suddenly one of my sons, his eyes filled with tears, reached out and put his arms around me. "Dad, I love you so much," he cried. "I'm so grateful you're my dad and that we can be together as a family." Those next few moments, when I in turn shared my feelings about him, were some of the most tender of my life.

As I shared this experience later with my wife, we felt as if we were in on a great secret. This was what life was all about—developing close, loving relationships and sharing those feelings with each other. What if my son had repressed those feelings because he thought boys weren't supposed to show emotion? That moment made the thousands of hours we'd invested in our children worth it. Whether we recognize it, whether we are willing to admit it, that is what we all hunger for: the feeling of closeness to others, beginning with our Heavenly Father—the feeling of loving, appreciating, and prizing others and of being loved, accepted, and valued ourselves.

One night when I was down on the floor playing with my boys, one young son said, "Dad, thank you for playing with us like this. It's really a lot more fun when you're here." That statement was a double thank-you. I not only felt appreciated, I could see that my son was learning to be in touch with his feelings and express them.

As I look back over my life, the memories that really stand out are those times I've shared my true feelings of love with others and they've shared theirs with me. My father has been dead for years now, but I can still hear his voice in my mind saying, "I love you, son" or "I'm proud of you, son." It's a thrilling thing when couples and families can throw off their taboos about showing emotions and can communicate about their feelings, when they listen and speak to each other with sensitivity, and when they—sometimes for the first time—experience intimacy. I'll never forget one man who came to believe that sharing his feelings was a sign of strength, not weakness, and told his wife how he'd been feeling about himself. Seeing her receive his words with gratitude and relief and understanding, he exclaimed with the light of discovery in his face, "It's a whole new world, isn't it!"

That's the point. The world of feelings is an exciting world, the place where we really live, the home of our testimonies and joys and sorrows—all of the things that make us uniquely human.

C. Richard Chidester, *father of eight, is employed in the Church Educational System as associate area director for Davis County, Utah. He is currently the Scoutmaster in the Bountiful Sixteenth Ward.*

Developing Sensitivity in Marriage

Both men and women can struggle with insensitivity, but it can be overcome with awareness, empathy, and consideration.

By David H. Coombs

I had to go to an early morning faculty meeting some thirty minutes away from home. Since it was Relief Society day, too, and we had only one car, I promised my wife, Marva, the Relief Society nursery leader, that I would be home in time to help her get our preschoolers and all the nursery materials to the meeting on time. But things just didn't go as planned. First, my meeting ran late. And then I remembered I had a counseling appointment with a student. So I called Marva to inform her that I wouldn't be home to help and that she would have to call someone else for a ride.

"Honey," I said, "I'm sorry, but I know you would want me to keep my commitment with my student. You do understand, don't you?"

She could have reluctantly agreed with me, burying her feelings of resentment and pretending that it would be all right. Instead, being honest with her feelings and with me, she said, "David, I really want you to keep your commitment with me! I need the car, and I need your support. So won't you please call your student and re-schedule the appointment?" I did as she requested, grateful for a wife who tells me her feelings while still being sensitive to mine.

Thinking of that experience later, I realized what I had done.

Having made a commitment to her, I seemed ready at the drop of a hat to break it. Without knowing it, I was telling her that my work was more important than hers, and that if there was to be a sacrifice, she would be the one to make it. Of course, I didn't say it in those words, and I would have been shocked if she had accused me of implying that. But when I considered it afterward, I concluded that that was really the message I was giving her and that I was being insensitive to some very real needs.

I've noticed this problem—self-centeredness and insensitivity—over and over in my work as a professional marriage counselor and as director of an LDS institute. The problem is a real one, and it isn't unique to one sex. Both men and women struggle with it. But it can be overcome—with a little awareness, empathy, and consideration.

I think men are especially susceptible to insensitivity because in our society they generally have more power than women: more education, more income, more control of public and business finances, more leadership positions in business and government. And in the Church, they are given the priesthood and are told to be the patriarch and to preside in the home. If men are not careful they can misuse this power and become insensitive and selfish. Some LDS men have a tendency to rule over their wives in a dominating way (see D&C 121:39). Others, operating on the false premise that women are seriously lacking in wisdom, judgment, or common sense, become sarcastic and critical of their wives. They won't admit to having such a negative view of women—they may even be found intellectualizing about the greatness of womankind. But their behavior speaks even louder.

At an elders quorum party that Marva and I attended early in our marriage, I told some cute jokes on her and also a few mother-in-law jokes—all, of course, at their expense. It seemed innocent enough to do because the others were doing it too. But when we got home, Marva told me how embarrassed and hurt she was, and she requested that all jokes and personal experiences shared publicly be positive and complimentary. When I considered my behavior, I agreed that I had no cause to belittle her or her mother—that derogatory jokes about women are unnecessary and avoidable. Hers was a reasonable request: again, I was glad she pointed out my insensitivity sensitively—and early in our marriage.

The role of homemaker is also a frequent target of men's criticism and jokes. I've heard men say, "Women have it easy; they don't have to worry about all the problems of making a living." This may be said in jest, but it still sounds critical, discounting the role of the woman in the home. We husbands should never make our wives feel that their work is small, unimportant, or of less worth than ours. Their job at home is every bit as important as our job of making a living. And just as husbands need to feel that their wives appreciate their role as provider, wives need the same appreciation from their husbands for their work as homemaker.

We have a desk in our bedroom which my wife uses for her church work and for other activities. I frequently find myself reminding her to keep it cleared off and orderly. On one occasion when I was tired, hungry, and angry about something else, I used the cluttered desk as an excuse to vent my angry feelings. Demanding in a rather offensive manner that she immediately clean it off, I let her know that since she's home all day she could have taken a few minutes to work at it.

She responded by gently leading me over to the closet to show me all the shirts she had washed and ironed that day, then to my dresser drawers to show me all the clean clothes she had washed and folded neatly away. She calmly reminded me of the sick children she had cared for and taken to the doctor, and of the good dinner she had ready for me when I came home. Then she said, "Honey, what I need from you is not criticism for what I haven't done, but expressions of appreciation for what I *have* done. Then I'll feel more like working at my desk." I apologized, she accepted, I expressed appreciation, she cleaned her desk, and we concluded happily.

Besides verbally expressing our appreciation, we husbands can and should *demonstrate* our feelings of the worth of our wives' work at home by helping them out with it. By rolling up our sleeves and changing diapers, mopping and vacuuming floors, and washing dishes alongside our wives, we can show them that we consider their work important and valuable—not demeaning or condescending—and that we're grateful for what they do for us.

Women can fall into the trap of insensitivity as easily as men can. My wife, Marva, tells me that too often women's conversations about their husbands are concluded with the phrase, "Well, you know how men are," implying that men are just big little boys or that they are demanding and tyrannical. Just as some men are guilty of uncomplimentary jokes and criticism about their wives, some women complain endlessly about their husbands. And when they hear good ideas in Relief Society or elsewhere that could increase the quality of their marriage or the spirituality in their home, they say, "If I did that, he'd just laugh," or "He'll never do it." They seem to have little faith in their husbands and expect little from them. "I know the way some women can talk about their husbands," Marva says. "I wonder if the whiny, critical complaints I hear publicly are not just the iceberg tip of much insensitivity to each other in these marriages."

I appreciate Marva's directness in handling problems that may arise between us. She would never knowingly hurt me. When she is hurt, she assumes it is unintentional—and so she deals with the problem instead of attacking the person. Instead of lashing out with accusations, striking at my pride and engendering anger, she focuses on the problem: "When you came home late today, it really hurt me because I had planned to. . . ." Then I'm not personally offended and am more likely to respond sensitively. Marva has a good philosophy: "Just as Johnny Lingo, by his expectations, was able to have an 'eight-cow-wife,' " she says, "each woman can have her own 'Six Million Dollar Man.' It takes charity, the pure love of Christ. We have to love unconditionally, to forgive and be forgiven, to expect the best, and to never stop doing our best."

Family finances can cause hurt feelings unless both parties are sensitive to each other. I recall hearing about a husband who required his wife to list each item of clothing she wished to purchase, along with its price. Only after he approved her list would he give her a check to cover the items. Then she could go back and actually purchase the clothes. In some cases the problem is reversed, and wives become critical of their husbands' use of the family funds.

I trust my wife's judgment and I want her to know it. So we discuss our finances, go over our budget, and decide together what we can afford. Then we trust each other to stay within the limits we've agreed upon. And when problems arise, it's easier to handle them sensitively.

Recently I wanted to buy a new, expensive car, and after a very persuasive salesman had convinced me I deserved it (I must admit I was very cooperative), I went home and announced to my wife what I was going to do. Expecting to have to defend my idea, I was ready with my arguments. She responded with some concern about the wisdom of buying such an expensive car, but then said, "Honey, I trust you and I know you wouldn't do it unless you really thought it was the best thing to do." Feeling very keenly my responsibility to act wisely, I couldn't go through with it. I had to live up to the expectation my wife had of me. She could have criticized me and discounted my idea, but instead, she sensitively let me know how she felt and then expressed confidence that I would handle my stewardship well. I've often thought that was a good example of dealing with differences in a positive way—without making each other feel defensive and resentful. And I'm grateful for the many other times Marva has shown me that sensitivity is better medicine for marriage than criticism born of self-centeredness.

I don't like win-lose situations between husbands and wives because just as the name implies, one wins at the expense of the other. In reality, both lose: the "winner" has an unhappy and resentful spouse. But by avoiding negative criticism and by being sensitive to each other, every couple can negotiate win-win solutions.

Sensitivity is also an important element in the affectional aspect of marriage. As a marriage counselor, I've seen marital insensitivity appear in two forms: selfish demands and selfish denials of affection. Regarding selfish demands of affection, I'm convinced that as husbands are thoughtful and sensitive to the tender feelings of their wives, as they conscientiously court their wives and strive to make them feel loved and cherished, they will find feelings of selfishness and self-centeredness fade. And regarding selfish denials of affections, a female client once complained to me, "Maybe after a few years of daily assurance of my husband's love, I wouldn't need it much after that." All she really needed was the assurance that every successful marriage is dependent upon—daily nourishment such as a hug, kiss, kind words, expressions of acceptance, acts of service, words of appreciation, and many "I love yous."

Another client said to me, "Of course I love my wife. But do I have to tell her all the time?" I tried to help him see that although he might be satisfied with a minimum of emotional expression, his wife obviously wasn't, and that for her sake, as well as his, he should reconsider his point of view and unselfishly make his wife feel the love that he really had for her.

The most important messages husbands and wives can give each other daily are that they are each other's best friend, that they love and cherish one another, that each respects and appreciates the other's work, and that no one is more important to them. These messages, conveyed in act as well as word, are products of selflessness and sensitivity.

David H. Coombs, a professional marriage and family therapist, serves as Scout advisor for his Orange, California, stake.

Getting to Know You Better

A Marriage Quiz

By Brent A. Barlow

Some time ago I taught a priesthood lesson on marriage. At the end I said, "Wouldn't it be interesting if we would all go home and do two things: (1) ask our wives how we could be better husbands, and (2) listen to what they have to say." After priesthood meeting I returned home and began eating a late breakfast. My wife, Susan, asked about my lesson, and between bites of cereal I indicated that as far as I could tell it went pretty well.

"What did you say?" she asked. I took another spoonful of cereal and replied, "I told them to go home and ask their wives how they could be better husbands, and then listen to their comments." I chuckled. "I'll bet some of them are having some pretty interesting discussions right now." I took another sip of orange juice. Susan walked over to the kitchen counter and was rather quiet as I continued to enjoy my breakfast. After a few minutes she said, "Do you really want to know?"

"Know what?" I asked.

"How you could be a better husband," she replied. "You do follow your own advice, don't you?"

Suddenly I lost my appetite. I put down my toast, and she

began. It was not so much what I was doing that concerned her, she said, but what I could be doing that would greatly improve our marriage. I listened. Our discussion had lasted about an hour when the phone rang. Susan answered it and talked for a minute or two and hung up.

"Who was it?" I asked.

"It was Brother Larson," she replied. "He said he would be a little late picking you up to go home teaching."

Susan walked out of the kitchen and called back, "He said he and his wife were having some sort of discussion. Something to do with what you said in priesthood meeting this morning."

As husbands and wives, how well *do* we know each other? Most of us knew enough about our spouse at one time to agree to marriage. But what have we learned about each other since then? People—and consequently marriages—change as the years go by. Some husbands and wives are surprised to find that there are still things to learn about each other, even after several years of marriage. Some mistakenly believe that because they live together in the same house, they'll automatically know each other. Others assume that they each share the same perspective of their marriage—that since they are "one," they think exactly alike, enjoy exactly the same things, and derive exactly the same satisfaction from their relationship. And some even erroneously assume that because they love each other, each will always know what the other is thinking or feeling, so there's no need to express thoughts and sentiments.

Whatever the reasons, dialogue is infrequent or missing in too many marriages. Elder Hugh B. Brown has written: "Where there is deep and mature love, which is being nurtured and jealously guarded, *the couple will confide in each other and discuss all matters of joint interest—and in marriage everything should be of interest to both*—they will stand together in adversity, will lean on, support, and give strength to each other. They will find that their combined strength is more than double the strength of either one of them alone." (*You and Your Marriage*, Salt Lake City: Bookcraft, 1960, p. 30.)

To assist in marital communication, try the following exercise together. Allow yourselves sufficient time when there will be no interruptions. You might wish to divide the exercise into several sessions, considering two or three statements at each session. First, respond individually *in writing* to the statements. Then exchange papers and talk about what you've written. Don't try to review your responses simultaneously. While one of you is reading or speaking, the other should listen or ask clarifying questions. Then switch roles.

Complete the following statements:

1. In our marriage, I feel loved when you . . .
2. In our marriage, I feel appreciated when you . . .
3. In our marriage, I am happiest when . . .
4. In our marriage, I am saddest when . . .
5. In our marriage, I am angriest when . . .
6. In our marriage, I would like more . . .
7. In our marriage, I would like less . . .
8. In our marriage, I feel awkward when . .
9. In our marriage, I feel uneasy when . . .
10. In our marriage, I feel excited when . . .
11. In our marriage, I feel close to you when . . .
12. In our marriage, I feel distant from you when . . .
13. In our marriage, I feel most afraid when . . .
14. My greatest concern/fear about our marriage is . . .
15. What I like most about myself is . . .
16. What I dislike most about myself is . . .
17. The feelings that I have the most difficulty sharing with you are . . .
18. The feelings that I can share most easily with you are . . .
19. Our marriage could be greatly improved with just a little effort if we . . .
20. The one thing in our marriage that needs the most attention is . . .
21. The best thing about our marriage is . . .

Brent A. Barlow, associate professor in the Department of Family Sciences, Brigham Young University, is the father of seven children and serves on the high council in the Orem Northeast Stake.

RESOLVING DIFFERENCES

A Change of Heart: Key to Harmonious Relationships

The keys to peace and harmonious relationships are found within our personal application of basic gospel principles.

By C. Richard Chidester

I once counseled a man whose outlook and behavior were so accusing that he frequently swore at his wife and children with the vilest of swear words. I met with him and his wife for a couple of sessions, trying to help him understand and overcome his accusing mentality. But he took offense, called me names, and stormed out of my office. His wife subsequently asked for a separation, and he ended up living with his parents. I never expected to see the couple again.

Needless to say, I was shocked almost beyond belief when he called me on the phone two months later and said he was ready for more counseling! After apologizing for his former behavior, he explained what had been happening to him. Staying with his parents had helped him see himself more clearly. As he watched them continuously put each other down and accuse and strike out at each other, he began to realize that he had been acting just like they had always done. Soon he hated to go home at night because of his parents' behavior. He also became more aware of the same accusing behavior in others, especially the people he worked with. He observed that his colleagues spent much of the day gossiping and complaining and putting each other down. As he began to miss his family, his heart gradually began to soften, and he felt remorse for the way he had treated them. Scenarios of the times he had physically and verbally abused his wife and children flashed through his mind, and he became haunted by the need to make up for his intolerable behavior. His sorrow increased until he began to feel that it was almost more than he could bear.

When he came to me for help, it was obvious that he was experiencing a change of heart. For the first time, he was admitting to himself how awful his behavior had been. Of course, he had really known it all along. But he had deceived himself into believing that his wife, children, and circumstances were to blame for his misery and unhappiness. He had convinced himself that if people only understood him better and were more compassionate he wouldn't have had the problems he did. Caught in a paralyzing web of misery and self-pity, he had failed to see himself as the architect of that web.

But now he was beginning to see the truth about himself. That self-knowledge took him down into the depths of humility with a broken heart and a contrite spirit; he acknowledged his need to change and sought the Lord's help in improving. Now he could see that his problems were *spiritual* and *of his own making*. He also saw that *he* was in the best position to do something about them. He was ripe for change. As he responded to the workings of the Spirit within him, his heart continued to soften. It didn't take many sessions of counseling or much prompting from others for him to make positive and lasting changes.

This man's turnabout was the most dramatic I have ever seen in a client. I'll be forever grateful to him for confirming to me what the Lord has said all along through the scriptures and the prophets, but which so many of us fail to understand: *The keys to peace and harmonious relationships are to be found within our personal application of the basic principles of the gospel.* In other words, in order to have peace and harmony in our relationships, we must first have peace and harmony within ourselves. Such peace comes when we are doing what we know to be right by following the still small voice of the Spirit.

This message is taught by most bishops, one way or another, when counseling members, but it is sometimes ignored in favor of behavior modification techniques. The world suggests that we can manufacture our own change by goal-setting, behavioral objectives, behavior change techniques, positive mental attitude, and various other forms of self-improvement programs. Although these approaches may be useful in bringing about a measure of desired behavioral change, they are only partial because they are terrestrial. They are the best man can produce by himself.

The Lord has made it abundantly clear in the scriptures that the mighty change in our nature that really needs to take place can be done only by God through the principles of his gospel. (See Helaman 3:35.) The Lord's promise is that when our hearts become broken and our spirits contrite, he will change our natures and purify our hearts. Then we will have "no more disposition to do evil, but to do good continually." (Mosiah 5:2.) Such a state of righteousness will lead to harmonious relationships, because in that state we don't "have a mind to injure one another." (Mosiah 4:13.)

What does it mean to have a broken heart and a contrite spirit? A broken heart comes from recognizing with deep godly sorrow that Jesus Christ, who was pure and holy and deserved no punishment for sin, took upon himself the punishment for all of our sins so that we might be spared from suffering for them. Truly recognizing the magnitude of his suffering for us individually is a humbling, heartbreaking experience; it should motivate us to change and to return his love. In addition, a broken heart includes feeling genuine sorrow for our individual sins and for the suffering they cause ourselves and others.

To have a contrite spirit means to have a penitent spirit. After recognizing our fallen state as mortals (see Mosiah 4:5), we seek the Lord in a repentant spirit and plead with him for a new heart and for forgiveness and mercy through the atoning blood of Christ. As we exercise faith in Christ and dependence on him, he will help us change. Through genuine heartfelt repentance, we truly recognize and concentrate on our own wrongdoings and on our need for improvement, rather than on how much others need to improve. Then, as we seek forgiveness and the mercy of Christ, pleading for his help, his Spirit will change our hearts and give us the moment-to-moment guidance we need so we can live Christlike lives. In this way, the Spirit of God changes us from our fallen, self-sufficient, proud state to a condition where we can live Christlike lives and achieve a state of righteousness.

It would be convenient if there were a magic formula or a slick technique for finding happiness other than through these principles of the gospel. But there isn't. However, both ecclesiastical and professional counselors regularly see people who want peace and harmonious relationships without repenting of unloving behavior. They want peace and a righteous heart through secularism instead of through the sanctifying influence of the Spirit of God. I am beginning to learn how true the Savior's statement was when he said, "Peace I leave with you, my peace I give unto you: not as the world giveth, give I unto you." (John 14:27.)

Mercy—Instead of "Justice"

When people aren't getting along, they are usually caught up in a blame-blame cycle where each sees the other as the problem, as the one who needs to change. They want to see "justice" done—which usually means they want justice done in their behalf *against* the other person. This kind of "justice" is really revenge. When we are out for revenge we blame, accuse, and provoke others to wrath—and then we blame them for it. Only when we quit seeing each other in such self-justifying ways can lasting, substantial changes take place. In other words, it is not until we quit looking to the other for change, begin to be honest about ourselves, and take responsibility for our own behavior that a change of heart can take place. Honesty about our own weaknesses leads to a more compassionate view of others.

On one occasion I was trying to help a woman see her husband more truthfully and compassionately instead of so accusingly. I told her I would begin describing her husband and his situation as I saw them, and then I would ask her to take over and continue with her own observations. I began by mentioning some of his problems and limitations, and then started enumerating his strengths. Then I asked her to take over. She described how good he was with the children, how helpful he was in the ward, how much he generally liked people.

Suddenly she looked at me with shock on her face. "Do you

know what I see? I see the man I married!" I explained that he had been there all along, but that she had ceased to see his strengths because of her exaggerated attention to his weaknesses. She then looked at her husband, and as her head fell onto his shoulder she sobbed, "I'm so sorry for the way I have blamed you and treated you all these years. Can you ever forgive me?" She had come into that session feeling sorry for herself and for the way her husband had mistreated her. But she left sorrowing over the way *she* had treated *him*. As she admitted the truth to herself, her heart softened, leading her to a sincere desire to change.

When we are more concerned about our own attitude and behavior than those of others, improvements in relationships can begin to take place. We cannot force others to change, to be good, or to be more responsible; they have free will to act the way they want to. The real issue is how we react to them! Are we being compassionate, forgiving, and patient—or are we concentrating on whether they are being responsible or not? And the strength to act consistently the way we should, given our weaknesses, comes by actively seeking the Spirit of God. The doctrines of men emphasize only self-control, which provides partial help at best. The gift of the Spirit is where our real strength lies.

When this woman admitted to herself and to her husband how accusing and unforgiving she had been, she opened the door for him to be more truthful about his own weaknesses. If neither side in a conflict will back down, a stalemate exists. The only way to break a stalemate is for one or the other—preferably both—to initiate change by taking responsibility for his own part of the problem and suggesting ways he can change to make things better. Waiting for the other to make the first move or trying to accuse the other into changing only perpetuates the conflict.

Giving—and Receiving—Mercy

When we live by the law of "justice" (as generally interpreted by mankind to mean "revenge"), we are very exacting and demanding of others. And when they don't live up to our expectations, we take offense and want to punish them in compliance. Our suppressed awareness of our own sins and shortcomings traps us into accusing, self-righteous behavior. However, by coming down into the depths of humility, realizing our own weaknesses and turning to the Lord daily for forgiveness and guidance, we can have his Spirit with us—and harmonious relationships can follow. As we receive the Lord's mercy, it becomes more and more obvious how much we need it. Then, in turn, we feel the need to extend this mercy to others—being as compassionate and quick to forgive as the Lord is with us. This doesn't mean we won't have honest disagreements or differences, but we seek to resolve them honestly and straightforwardly—and unaccusingly.

I learned an important lesson on giving and receiving mercy one winter when my son Rob was taking care of the neighbors' rabbits. One night he forgot to empty the watering bottles—and the bottles were frozen solid the next morning. When he discovered his mistake, I had no mercy and became upset at his forgetfulness. I unjustly reproved him for forgetting and for making us both late that morning. After I arrived at work, my conscience wouldn't leave me alone. In a moment of truth I admitted to myself that Rob had made a simple human error similar to ones I frequently make. I admitted to myself that I had no justification in taking offense at his mistake, given my own weaknesses. The truth is, Rob is a conscientious boy who does many things well. My sorrow for my own wrongdoing motivated me to find him at school and apologize. I found that he had taken the whole thing compassionately; even though I had been wrong, he had seen it from my point of view and had taken no offense.

The experience greatly humbled me. If my heart had been right in the first place, I never would have become upset by Rob's simple mistake. If Rob hadn't been merciful, he could have taken my behavior personally, which could have harmed his own self-esteem as well as our relationship. After I had apologized (part of my repentance), a peace of conscience came like that which came to King Benjamin's people as they admitted their wrongdoing and called upon the Lord for forgiveness. (See Mosiah 4:3.)

Seeing Others Compassionately

In trying to help couples begin to see each other with

compassion and mercy rather than with "revenge" and accusations, I use the following exercise. It helps them see how the attitudes in our hearts determine the way we relate to others. A number of bishops I know have found the exercise useful in their counseling.

I ask each partner to close his or her eyes, and I close mine too so we don't distract each other. Then I say something like this:

"Think of all the things your mate has done that bother you—things you haven't liked, offensive mannerisms or traits, ways he or she has accused you or put you down. Take a minute to make a mental list. [One-minute pause.]

"Next, in your imagination, destroy that list somehow. Burn it, bury it, or throw it in the garbage. Destroy it so it is gone forever.

"Next, begin to think of the trials, challenges, or difficulties your mate is facing in life. Take about thirty seconds to ponder what he or she is going through and what it must be like for him or her to face those challenges. [Thirty-second pause.]

"Next, think of the positive qualities, traits, and attributes of your husband or wife—the things you and others admire, the things that impressed you when you were courting. [Thirty-second pause.]

"Now, ponder the good times you have had together over the years—times you felt positive, loving or close; times you laughed together or needed to support and help each other; times you went through something significant together, such as the birth of a child. [Thirty-second pause.]

"Now, open your eyes. As you do, get in touch with the feelings or attitudes you are having in your heart toward your spouse. What are those feelings?"

So far without exception when couples have been genuine in going through this exercise—whether they did it with each other or toward their children—they have ended up feeling greater compassion, understanding, warmth, forgiveness, kindness, or love. Many have felt sorrowful for having been so unkind. They realize that when they see the other through the eyes of honesty and mercy, they see a different person than when they are seeing accusingly through the eyes of revenge. They realize how much of the time they spend meting out revenge, and how little they are seeing each other in a positive, merciful light.

I recall one particularly touching incident. After completing this experience, a husband looked over at his wife and said, "How can I ever repay you for the way you have loved me, sacrificed for me and the children, and forgiven me when I have been so selfish?"

When we have the Spirit in abundance and are perceiving reality honestly and accurately, we realize that all mortals are a composite of strengths and weaknesses. Given our own frailties, we have little occasion to take offense at their mistakes. As we realize this, our hearts become broken and our spirits contrite, and we begin to treat others compassionately.

The Book of Mormon gives numerous examples of people's hearts changing from a carnal, selfish state to a state of righteousness. That change always came as a gift of God, through faith and sincere repentance. It was not something the people were able to manufacture by their own strength. "They did fast and pray oft, and did wax stronger and stronger in their humility, and firmer and firmer in the faith of Christ, unto the filling of their souls with joy and consolation, yea, even to the purifying and the sanctification of their hearts, which sanctification cometh because of their *yielding their hearts unto God.*" (Helaman 3:35; italics added.)

We, too, can change our behavior through faith in Christ and repentance. The sanctifying influence of the Spirit of God can change our natures or our personalities so that we become "a saint through the atonement of Christ the Lord." (Mosiah 3:19.) And the marvelous thing about it is that when we have the Spirit of God in abundance, we may have the attendant fruits of the Spirit—some of which are love, joy, peace, long-suffering, gentleness, goodness, faith, meekness, and temperance. (See Galatians 5:22-23.) And when our own hearts have changed, our relationships with others will improve.

C. Richard Chidester, father of eight, is employed in the Church Educational System as associate area director for Davis County, Utah. He is currently the Scoutmaster in the Bountiful Sixteenth Ward.

The Compassionate Marriage Partner

The proper foundation of forgiveness, compassion, and charity will bring peace and harmony to a home.

By Terrance D. Olson

We were packing for a short trip to the mountains of northern New Mexico, and I was loading the last of the children and supplies into the car. My wife appeared at the door and said cheerfully, "Well, we're all set!" As she was pulling the locked door closed, I realized I didn't have my keys! I yelled quickly, "*DON'T SHUT THAT door*." Too late. In an instant I was irritated. I said to my wife, implying she was to blame, "My *keys* are in the *house*!"

Fortunately, a forgotten open window allowed us access to the house without the loss of much time, and my feelings dissipated. I "forgave" my wife for having caused me emotional pain. Later, as I thought of the experience, I realized I had found it convenient to blame my wife because it was a way of justifying my own failure. By my hostile feelings I could make it appear that *she* was the guilty one and that I was a helpless victim.

The truth is that my irritation was not due to her behavior at all. It was, instead, the product of my own unwillingness to accept the responsibility of my actions, and obviously, she hadn't needed my forgiveness—but I certainly needed hers.

The real issue was my need to repent of the feelings I had.

Had she been in some kind of transgression, then the solution to the problem would have been for her to repent and me to forgive. In this case, however, only my repentance was necessary to restore us to oneness. I understood also that my repentance, my giving up of my feelings of resentment, would have been necessary whether she had been guilty of anything or not. I saw that I could not be both unrepentant (or unforgiving) and compassionate at the same time. These are two incompatible attitudes.

This almost trivial incident illustrates some important truths about forgiveness, charity, and compassion. I've learned that these Christlike attitudes are the foundation for dealing with the big problems as well as the little ones that may beset a marriage. They can lead to oneness in even the most strained relationships.

As a marriage and family therapist, I occasionally meet people who feel that problems in their marriage are much too large to ever be resolved. Sister Flagg (not her real name) was one of them. She shared with me her feelings of helplessness about being in a loveless marriage. When I asked her to imagine her life one year from now and to describe what her marriage would be like then, her expression shifted from discouragement to despair. She was sure her marriage could never be different. She doubted she could ever love her husband; he was aloof, uncaring, wrapped up in his own world. He rarely took time for her—for *them*. He wasn't physically abusive, but was distant from her.

I saw the following as features of her situation: (1) She felt helpless in the face of what she saw as a hopeless situation. (2) She was emotionally burdened by the isolation from her husband. (3) She was convinced that she was a victim of circumstances, that she was trapped and miserable because of her husband's actions. (4) She saw the gospel as a nice set of ideals that didn't adequately address her circumstances. (It was as if she were insisting that her brand of suffering was an exception to the application of gospel principles.)

I am convinced that the gospel of Jesus Christ is the solution—a very practical one—to problems in marriage. Even though some husbands and wives see scriptural counsel as too "abstract" or too "idealistic," I see continually how the gospel is the source of personal and marital happiness and that it has the answers to solving problems in marriage.

Consequently, I sought to explain to Sister Flagg how three important gospel attitudes—forgiveness, charity, and compassion—could help her and her husband resolve their difficulties. I tried to help her see that just as I felt that my wife had "caused" my irritation when I was locked out of the house, Sister Flagg was unjustly blaming her husband for "causing" her misery. Whether my wife had been guilty or not, I was wrongly accusing her of causing my reaction. My feelings of resentment were my way of refusing to feel compassion for my wife. Sister Flagg was in a similar position: whether her husband was guilty or not, her feelings of helplessness were a way of showing how impossible it was for her to view him compassionately.

Now, I am not saying that her husband was innocent, that the solution to her problem was easy, or that the problem was "just in her head." I am suggesting, however, that her way of viewing her circumstances was part of the problem. By insisting she was helpless, she was producing hopelessness.

Suppose Brother Flagg was, indeed, as aloof and uncaring as Sister Flagg said he was, that everything she reported was true. By living gospel principles, she could still do much to improve her situation. Although there is no guarantee that her husband would respond and change, she could still rid herself of her bondage of helplessness and despair, and create a better life for herself and, hopefully, for her husband as well.

If people in Sister Flagg's position were to realize that *they* can do something about their problems, they would have begun to solve the problem. I remember working with a man who, like Sister Flagg, felt helpless; he was sure that nothing he could do would change the problems in his marriage. Although his feelings of helplessness were real, they were *not* produced by his situation; rather, he had produced them himself as a way of showing who was to blame. They were his "proof" that he could do nothing about his circumstances except be defeated by them. Harboring these feelings was his way of achieving vengeance against his wife for her "wrongs."

What could he do about these feelings? Like Sister Flagg, he could give them up in favor of the Christlike attitudes of forgiveness, charity, and compassion. He can't feel both helpless and forgiving simultaneously; he can either continue to insist he is helpless, or turn his heart to the Lord—and begin to solve the problem.

Our hostile feelings toward another person are more fundamental to our problems than that person's behavior. What others do to us does not render us uncompassionate or unforgiving. We do that to ourselves by refusing to forgive. Our road to personal peace requires our own repentance of those feelings of resentment.

Consider Doctrine and Covenants 64:10: "I, the Lord, will forgive whom I will forgive, but of you it is required to forgive all men." An attitude of forgiveness toward our companion is an important beginning. By having faith in the first two commandments, we are blessed by them. By loving the Lord with all our heart, we see our situation differently. By loving our husband or wife as ourselves, we see him or her more compassionately, and are no longer in despair. We are traveling on a gospel road, rather than on a path which denies the gospel.

Our emotional burden will be lifted as we realize that we aren't helpless. This is faith—not the kind of faith that lies passively on a shelf or hidden in a book—but the kind that *works* in the hearts and minds and lives of people. One gift of the gospel is the faith that God is neither a stranger to sorrow nor indifferent to our challenges. As we turn to gospel fundamentals in this way, we will give up the burden of our feelings of helplessness in exchange for faith. Although we will still have feelings, they will be of a different quality altogether than the despair we felt before.

"But," some may say, "that doesn't change the fact that we are victims. Haven't our companion's actions made it impossible for us to feel any other way than we now feel?"

The gospel teaches us that we are free "to act for [ourselves] and not be acted upon, . . . and all things are given [us] which are expedient." (2 Nephi 2:26-27.) In other words, whatever our spouse's attitudes or sins might be, his or her behavior is not sufficient to render us incapable of living as we feel we should.

Of course there are no magic steps to follow. But imagine what might occur to a husband, for example, if he were to see his wife compassionately—if he were to see her "wrongdoing" with charity? Would he see *her* point of view, *her* misery? Would he recognize her self-justifying behavior? Would he ponder how the two of them could work together to overcome their difficulties? Would he see hope for the future? The gospel answer to these questions is yes.

With a new attitude like this, we would be "free" to produce a better marriage. Instead of insisting that we are trapped, we would see an opportunity to be persuasive, gentle, meek, kind—to offer "love unfeigned" to each other. We would see our companions as the Lord sees them. We would have a new view of ourselves, of our husband or wife, and of our marriage—a view born of gospel living. We would become compassionate, rather than accusing, resentful, or despairing.

This change of heart is only the beginning; it won't change marriage problems overnight. But by seeing each other *compassionately*, we open the door to some effective problem-solving. Since power and influence really do come through an attitude of love unfeigned, of compassion and caring, we then can be a righteous influence in our marriage.

Of course, it is possible that our companion won't change and that we won't have the oneness in our marriage that we desire. But even if that happens, we can still be free of the bonds of resentment and hopelessness and can still find life meaningful and rewarding. We are not helpless; we are not victims of the situation.

Often, however, in situations like these, when one partner begins to live compassionately, many of the "problems" of the marriage partner disappear. When we are nursing grudges or harboring hostilities, the problems we see in our marriage partners are sometimes ones we have manufactured to justify our own resentments. When we repent of our own uncompassionate feelings, those resentments disappear and we see our loved ones in a new light. We then become the kind of compassionate marriage partners we wish our spouses were. And we can begin to play a role in blessing his or her life.

"Hereby perceive we the love of God," said John, "because he laid down his life for us: and we ought to lay down our lives for the brethren. But whoso hath this world's good, and seeth his brother [or husband, or wife, or child] have need, and shutteth up his bowels of compassion from him, how dwelleth the love of God in him? My little children, let us not love in word, neither in tongue; but in deed and in truth." (1 John 3:16-18.)

The gospel is the solution to problems in marriage. Changing our hearts by accepting the Atonement is a prerequisite to any change, including changes in marriages or families. We cannot decide what others will do, but the gospel of Christ, which includes forgiveness, charity, and compassion, is available to us. Because of it and our agency, we *can* decide what we will do. And since we reap the same spirit we sow, we can either lay a foundation of hostility and resentment, or we can sow the seeds of compassionate living as an invitation to peace and harmony in our homes.

Terrance D. Olson, professor of Family Sciences, Brigham Young University, and father of six children , serves as second counselor in the BYU Sixth Stake presidency and is a member of the Church Family Relations Writing Committee.

Winning the Argument or Solving the Problem

Which do you want?

By Steve Gilliland

As a bishop, a psychologist, and an institute director, I've had the opportunity to counsel or visit with dozens of couples who come in, trapped in a pattern of conflict they can't seem to break. The arguments, the quarrels, and the bickering feed into each other and the bitterness is heartbreaking. In my official capacities, I can usually be of help to them, but it was as a *husband* that I learned how to really help break the pattern.

Like many couples, Judy and I had our different points of view on such things as finances, decision making, family scheduling, etc. I reacted to our conflicts by trying to convince her that I was right and she was wrong. My college debate experience had sharpened my argumentative teeth and so it was easy to cut through her explanations and point out the errors in her logic. I usually won our arguments (or thought I had). But I noticed that our relationship was getting worse and worse. More and more often, our conversations would end with Judy in tears and unable to explain why. And I would have to face the fact that I, the great expert on how other people should solve their marital problems, wasn't doing so well with my own. For a long time, I believed it was all Judy's fault. After all, I was the authority—professionally and ecclesiastically. She was lucky to be married to an expert. She could have an audience with me whenever she wanted.

What I didn't understand until later was the depth of my own fear. What if it *wasn't* Judy's fault? What if *I* were wrong? That would mean I'd have to change. But change to what? How?

Our temple covenants challenged us to work out our problems instead of considering divorce as some of our friends had done. What moved me far enough to try something besides debating and lecturing was the real love and commitment we had for each other. And because I loved Judy so much, I was finally willing to sit on my own feelings and try to understand her rather than try to win the argument. When I stopped arguing and started listening, Judy started opening up.

But it was much more difficult to listen to my wife than a client. I was responsible for much of her pain and frustration. I was treating her like a child when I thought I was treating her like a companion. I viewed myself as being very rational and democratic. She saw me as being very defensive and authoritarian. It was hard for me to hear this kind of stuff. It couldn't be true (or could it?). True or not, the important thing was that this was how she perceived me.

It hurt to see my imperfections. My first reaction was to defend with my debate armament. It felt much better to win an argument than face my weaknesses. I was back on familiar ground. But Judy was closing up again. I felt more secure, but there was that wall between us—and I hated that wall. It was scary and painful to have her open up—but we felt closer. I saw strengths in her that I had never recognized before, and our love and respect grew.

I had a choice to make between security and closeness. I'm so glad I chose to risk. We drew closer together and that in itself was enough of a reward to keep trying. I really *was* doing something right. As we kept exploring, I realized that Judy had some great insights into *me*. Together we are still learning how to solve our problems and to stop worrying about winning arguments. It took us quite a while to realize what had been wrong with our first approach, and many of the couples I see are deadlocked in the same frustrating position.

In any conversation, there are two elements. The first one is the subject or the topic. The second one is the process—what the individuals are doing to each other in the discussion and how they are making each other feel.

Let me give you an example. One couple that came in for counseling subconsciously showed how the topic of their discussion was effectively demolished by the process. The husband, whom we'll call Jim, explained to me that they never seemed to find time to talk with each other anymore. Why?

"Well, there's church work and running the kids to activities almost every night."

At that, his wife, whom we'll call Mary, added "And there's your mother."

Jim admitted, "She does take a little of our time."

"A little!" exclaimed Mary. "She's always calling you to do this and that. Does she call your brothers and sisters? Does she call her home teachers? No."

"What does the Church tell us about taking care of our parents?" retorted Jim. "I never complain about *your* mother's cigarettes or cats. Do I complain when we go to her house? I think the two of you could learn a lot from my mom."

"According to *her* I could," said Mary bitterly, "She reminds me that I'm a poor wife and a worse mother every time I talk with her."

What had begun as the couple's request to help them find ways to spend quality time together had almost instantly escalated into a full-scale battle. Their words, which defined the *topic* of their discussion, missed the real issue. As we worked through their problems together, it turned out that Mary was trying to say, "I feel discouraged. Please pay more attention to me. I need your help and support." She didn't say it very clearly, but it was the best she could do at the moment.

In our marriages we need to look underneath the *expressed* problems to the *actual* problems. This is done by becoming aware of process, instead of subject matter. When we look at process in conversations we can almost always improve communication by paying attention to four steps:

1. Try to understand your partner's point of view. Focus on what your spouse is trying to tell you, not on how you can make him change his mind. You don't have to agree, but listen.

2. What's happening to feelings during the conversation?

Ask yourself, What am I doing to my partner? How am I making him or her feel? How is he or she making me feel? As your spouse talks, you may feel threatened and uneasy by what she or he says. You may not recognize this, but if you feel like correcting or defending, be careful. If you yield to these feelings you'll probably have an argument. Sit on them. I know it's not easy.

3. Try to understand your partner's feelings. In Jim's case, this would have meant asking himself how helping his mother instead of Mary was making Mary feel. How did his mother's criticism make Mary feel? And how was Mary feeling about herself right then?

4. Let your partner know that you're trying to understand. Repeat in your own words what he or she seems to be saying or feeling. Jim could probably have dampened the conflict if he'd said something like, "You think I should spend less time helping my mother?" "You really seem frustrated about this," or "You really seem discouraged."

Check your own reactions during an argument. If someone seems more interested in winning, do you really believe that he loves you? And are you willing to trust him with your real feelings? Generally, in such instances, people become defensive and combative. On the other hand, how do you feel about someone who looks you in the eye, listens to you, and hears not only your words but your feelings?

Even if there's enough openness so that we can share our feelings, many attempts at communication run smack into a roadblock: the temptation to give advice. Sometimes when Judy would start to cry after another of our futile debates, I would uneasily comfort her: "Come on, don't cry. It's not that bad." Basically, I was trying to tell her that she really shouldn't feel what she was feeling. Until I stopped responding to my own uneasiness about her tears and started responding to her pain, we got nowhere in trying to solve our problems.

Similarly, if Jim had listened to Mary share her discouragement, he could have said something like, "Don't feel discouraged. You're a wonderful wife and mother" or "Don't be angry. Mom means well," or "Count your blessings. Things could be worse." And probably any of those bits of advice would have pushed them straight back into the argument. It's normal to feel uneasy when your partner is expressing strong feelings, and this "advice" looks like a fast way to solve the problem so the feelings will disappear. Of course, it's not. Those feelings need to come out.

You may feel that you should do something, give some help. Being there and caring enough to listen without criticizing is usually needed much more than your advice. "Let every man be swift to hear, slow to speak, slow to anger." (James 1:19.)

A second roadblock is your partner's perceptions. It's not what we intend to say but how we are perceived that really counts. For instance, a major difference between Judy and me is how we perceive housework—what should be done and what has priority. I remember that I used to come home on Primary day and find dishes in the sink because Judy put her Primary lesson first. I, of course, could easily tell her how to be organized enough to get both jobs done—and would, thinking I was helping her. Judy, of course, would perceive me as an enemy attacking her, not as a source of help.

In fifteen years of marriage, I've learned that "helping" means pitching in and doing the dishes or getting the kids mobilized to put the laundry away after I've washed the clothes. And I've learned to adjust my priorities; I'd love to come home to a spotless house and sink blissfully into a chair to read for twenty minutes before dinner is served. Well, until our seven children are considerably older, that's simply not going to happen. Sometimes we've even stacked dirty dishes in the closet when we've been expecting company because other things—our children and our relationship with each other—are simply more important.

But how can you be sure that your partner is perceiving your intentions correctly? One way is to "show . . . forth afterwards an increase of love" (D&C 121:43) by simply asking, at the end of your attempt to understand him or her: "How did this make you feel?"

It takes courage and caring to ask that question. He or she may respond to the topic instead of to the process by saying, "I disagree with you." If you rise to the bait, the argument will begin all over again. Instead, focus on feelings: "I guess I made you feel bad?" Remember, you're not an expert on her intentions and feelings. If Jim makes judgments like: "You're only saying that because you're angry that mother doesn't like the way you discipline Terry," he's asking for an argument on how she really feels.

Both of these roadblocks to understanding each other are related to a third problem: in most arguments, both people are at fault. We've talked about Jim and what he could have done differently, but Mary made some mistakes too. She attacked Jim's mother, an act that would be almost certain to make anyone react negatively. As we probed what had happened in that particular counseling session, Mary quickly realized the problem she'd created and asked Jim, "It bothered you when I criticized your mother, didn't it?"

Jim answered defensively, "Yes. She's had a hard life, and I can't see why it bugs you that I take some time to help her."

Mary tried to clarify her feelings while still recognizing his: "I realize that you love her, but I guess what I'm trying to say is that *I'm* going through some rough times now and I really need your help."

Still angry, Jim snapped, "You don't know what rough times are. My mother. . . ."

I was proud of Mary. Instead of arguing about who was having the roughest time—her or Jim's mother—she kept the process in mind and answered, "What you just said really hurts. I need your *help* now, not a lecture. Please. . . ."

And Jim, realizing what had happened, dropped the argument like a hot potato: "I'm sorry," he apologized. "Please tell me what's bothering you."

A fourth roadblock to understanding the process of communication develops if we communicate one message with our words and another with our tone of voice, inflection, gestures, or loudness of voice. "You must have had a hard day" can mean two different things, depending on whether it is spoken with tenderness or a sneer. If you get the wrong response to your message, don't defend yourself by attacking your partner: "I didn't say that! You always misunderstand me." That's setting up another argument on the *topic*. Instead focus on the *process* and ask both yourself and your partner, "What did I say or do to make it come across that way?"

One of the hardest things to change is a relationship where conflict has become a habit. Such a habit isn't comfortable and it's not happy, but at least you know what to count on. I seem to talk to more wives than husbands because research shows that many husbands are afraid to come in for counseling, fearful that either the husband or the wife will be shown to be "right." However, the goal of the counselor is to help the couple improve the *process* they use—so that the two together can work on resolving their differences.

On the other hand, some wives who come in for counseling have been so brutalized by years of argument that they're not willing to let go of their perception of their mate. "He'll never change," they say. And others, sadly, have hoped for so long and been so repeatedly rebuffed in their attempts to communicate that they're not sure they can face the pain of trying again.

If you find yourself trapped in a cycle of arguments and you think you need some help breaking out of it, what can you do?

Go first to your bishop. He has the primary stewardship. However, a bishop may neither have the time nor feel comfortable counseling couples on their problems. He may feel inspired to direct you to someone else. In some areas, counseling from LDS Social Services is available and the bishop can refer a couple to someone who has been trained in marital counseling. But in other areas, these personnel are not available, or sometimes understaffing means that they cannot give every problem the kind of time it needs.

In those cases, most communities have professional help available, either through community, university, or private sources. As a bishop, I rejoice when someone will counsel and work with my people. In areas where I know of practitioners whose values are compatible with LDS standards, I feel good about referring couples to them. In other cases, I would advise the couple to carefully and prayerfully choose a trained marriage counselor who is willing to work with them within the values of the gospel, even though it may take a little shopping around to find the right person.

As for Judy and me, it's easy to sum up where we are after fifteen years of marriage. There's never enough time to do everything, and we continue to struggle with our priorities. We probably always will. But we sure feel great about our relationship.

Steve Gilliland, director of the Institute of Religion, California State University at Long Beach, and father of eight children, serves as Scoutmaster of the Lakewood, California, First Ward.

To Change Your Marriage, Change Yourself

We have been given the freedom and responsibility to control only one person—ourselves.

By Afton J. Day

I met an old high school friend recently, and naturally the conversation turned to husbands, homes, and children, all acquired since our last meeting. I was disturbed by the discouragement Ann showed through comments like "You know Johnny never was very active in the Church," and somewhat apologetically, "I've taken up drinking coffee now—Johnny does it, so I figure I might as well."

In a similar experience, a Sunday School teacher recommended a book designed to inspire improved family relations. "What's the use?" lamented one newly baptized member. "It won't work unless both of us read it, and my wife won't read anything I bring home from Church!"

The ideal family model discourages many members of the Church. To some, the mere mention of the celestial family, where father exercises the priesthood and adores his happy and supportive wife, arouses feelings of despair and sometimes hostility. Many people cannot identify with such a picture and usually decide either that their family is doomed to a terrestrial existence or that they must, consciously or not, reject the family member who apparently makes celestialization impossible.

Such rejection seems to be a subtle attempt to infringe upon that person's agency. We have all been given the freedom and responsibility to control only one person—ourselves. We are exhorted against exercising control over another. Yet at the same time we Church members are encouraged to inspire and influence. It seems, then, that the first step to positive action is to recognize what we can and should do and what would infringe upon the other's agency.

A marriage becomes stale, even bitter, when one or both partners fall into the paralyzing habit of reacting to an unpleasant situation instead of planning and working to bring about a pleasant one. When this happens, usually the following situations arise:

1. You may use your mate as an excuse for putting forth less than your best efforts. For example, "My wife never appreciates the little things I do for her, so why bother?" or "Jim doesn't seem to notice whether the house is clean or not, so why should I break my neck keeping house?"

2. You may choose an inefficent way to change things, like criticizing ("This carpet looks like it hasn't been cleaned for two years!"), complaining ("My husband doesn't show the least bit of interest in the Church. How I envy you women who have the priesthood in your home!"), rationalizing ("If I only had my wife's support, I would be an effective father."), threatening, bargaining, and issuing ultimatums. They may be honest reactions, but they are worthless ways to achieve goals.

If nagging, coercion, hinting, criticizing, complaining, rationalizing, and bargaining won't help us reach the goals in our homes, what will?

First, we must determine what goals in marriage are worthy ones. A happy home, a Christlike atmosphere, an environment conducive to growth and progress—these are all acceptable and deserve much time and effort. On the other hand, a goal that involves remaking your mate's personality to suit your specifications is not in keeping with the Savior's plan and almost certainly will result in lessening love and mutual respect, two musts in a celestial relationship.

Second, the key to all human relationships, whether parent-child, teacher-student, or husband-wife, is honest respect for the other individual. *Honest* respect, more than simply respect for the aspects of his or her personality that are pleasing to you, implies respect for a person's right to be himself, whatever that may be. With our understanding of the divine destiny of man and with our strict gospel standards, though that kind of respect may seem difficult at first, we know it is vital.

Third, we must avoid the "power struggle," a common stumbling block in the pursuit of good family relationships. Certainly no Latter-day Saint would knowingly become involved in a marital power struggle; we believe that the husband is definitely the head of the home and that the wife is to support him in righteousness. But somehow a part of most of us, without even letting our well-versed minds know what is happening, manages to engage us in a battle to win, to control, to gain power over another. The question of who should be responsible for emptying the trash, a problem of persistent sloppiness, or frequent disagreements over which friends to invite to dinner may be manifestations of the attempt by one partner to control and the equally determined resolve of the other to stand firm.

Once the power struggle climate has been established, the win-lose question becomes much more important than the original problem (emptying trash, neatness, choosing friends). Some couples play the "If You Mention It, It Won't Get Done" game. The husband will point out (he thinks matter-of-factly, the wife thinks harshly and accusingly) an area of the house that needs attention. First, the battle cry: ("When you get time, you need to clean this closet."), then the defense, expressed in thought only: ("How *dare* you question my housekeeping ability? I'll *never* clean that closet!"). The wife might find time to paper the living room, take the children to a movie, or polish the silver, but she will never find time to clean the closet. It remains untidy until the husband sullenly cleans it himself—an even greater insult, from the wife's point of view.

Who wins? No one, and communication becomes more and more strained and tempers become short. Even valuable senses of humor become less functional. When we played that game, I found an easy way out of our power struggle was for me to look around the house and ask myself what my husband would be most likely to ask me to do next, and then to do it. The first time he started to make a suggestion and then realized the job had already been done, I experienced positive feelings I hadn't had for years!

In a marriage, the power struggle which shows itself in problems as mundane as cleaning closets and emptying trash may just as easily manifest itself in matters of great import. Just as many wives react negatively to housekeeping suggestions, I have seen husbands and wives who felt the need to retain their freedom to decide whether or when to start attending church regularly, whether or when to stop smoking, or whether or when to listen to the missionaries. Sometimes when the pressure is removed and a feeling of "I respect your ability to decide what's best for you" replaces the "I know what's right" attitude, all members of the family can be more receptive to spiritual blessings.

But what about the responsibility we have to cry repentance? We know that a priesthood holder should govern the family; the scriptures say that the husband is the head of the wife, even as Jesus Christ is the head of the Church. (Ephesians 5:23.) Latter-day scripture, however, indicates that a priesthood holder should use extreme caution in the way he exercises his authority; he must avoid coercion or constraint in any form. (See D&C 121:37-39.) Women in the Church have often been admonished to "provoke" their husbands to good works. And even a superficial review of the scriptures and Church history indicates that we have every right and responsibility to remind and exhort. Yet Joseph Smith admonished the women of the Nauvoo Relief Society against nagging:

"You need not be teasing your husbands because of their deeds, but let . . . your innocence, kindness, and affection be felt. . . . Not war, not jangle, not contradiction, or dispute, but meekness, love, purity—these are the things that should magnify you in the eyes of all good men." (*Documentary History of the Church*, 4:605.)

Section 121 of the Doctrine and Covenants promises that the Holy Ghost will help worthy priesthood holders know how best to use the power of God in their dealings with others. (See D&C 121:43.) Nephi tells us that this privilege is not reserved for priesthood holders alone, but that the Holy Ghost "is the gift of God unto all those who diligently seek him." (1 Nephi

10:17.) And what a priceless gift this is, of especial need to those of us who have prejudices and habits to overcome.

I learned an important fourth principle of achieving goals in the home at a recent prospective elder's function. There we listened to the testimony of a man who two or three years ago would have been a tough contender in the "Least Likely to Become Interested in the Church" category. As he stood up, I recalled the afternoons I had spent listening to his wife, Nancy, tell of his lack of consideration for her and of his bitterness and cynicism toward the Church. This warm, likeable young man standing in front of us bore no resemblance to the person Nancy had once described. He told us how, several years earlier, their relationship had come to a stage that he described as "barely tolerable."

"It was really bad," he said. "I don't suppose we would have divorced—we both knew that would be a horrible thing to do to the kids—but I know we weren't doing them a lot of good together, either. Nancy used to bug me about joining the Church, setting an example for the children, and, oh, a lot of things; eventually she just got distant and sort of acted like I wasn't there. Although she did complain sometimes, I think she was just as relieved as I was when I'd find reasons to work late or take the kids somewhere, just to get out of the house.

"For some reason Nancy changed one day. All of a sudden she started acting as if she really cared about me, like doing little things for me the way she'd done when we were going together. At first I was suspicious—she'd had these spurts before, after she'd read an article or book or something, but they didn't last. This time she seemed pretty serious about it, and the really astonishing thing was that she didn't want any favors in return!"

We were impressed by his account of how things went from good to better and how his attitude had changed as a result of Nancy's behavior. He said something about its being a miracle, and I said a silent amen. Nancy had told me about the change in her. She said she realized one day how serious the situation had become, and she had done what she had learned to do when things appeared hopeless. In spite of the spiritual low she had reached in her personal attitude, she decided to share her problem with the Lord.

"I had read somewhere," she said, "that a vocal prayer was often more effective, and I needed all the advantages I could get. I prayed aloud, that afternoon locked in my room, more fervently and humbly than I had ever prayed before. I confessed that I knew the Lord was not pleased with our home and made known my desire to improve it. I pleaded with my Heavenly Father to help Stan to be more considerate and to help him understand about the gospel.

"Well, I'm not claiming to have heard a voice, or seen a vision, or anything, just a thought popping into my troubled mind. I believed at first my mind had wandered, and I was ashamed of my lack of concentration. But the thought, I'm sure now, wasn't mine. It had to be my answer, although goodness knows it was not at all the one I wanted! The idea was clear and powerful: 'When you're perfect, then we can start worrying about him!'

"As hard as it was to do, I felt compelled to make an all-out effort to be a better wife. I at least had to try! Then a second manifestation came one evening several months later as I sat in sacrament meeting. Something was said that focused my attention on a couple in the ward I had often admired, even envied, for their close and spiritual relationship. I was suddenly engulfed with a peaceful, nearly ecstatic feeling, and I *knew* I had the power within myself to make our home a holy and heavenly place.

"A sensation much, I suppose, like the burning that comes when someone is converted to the gospel told me that the Lord was watching, helping, working with Stan, and that he was pleased with Stan's efforts at work and in the community toward helping his fellowman. I understood, really understood that day, that my Heavenly Father had a tremendous love for my husband, and I felt so ashamed for the hostility I had felt."

Self-direction, respect for and acceptance of others, staying out of power struggles, openness to suggestion from the Holy Spirit. Simple? Very. I have used hundreds of words to say what the Savior said in eight: "Love one another, as I have loved you." (John 15:12.) Easy? Unfortunately not, but tasks that have such tremendous rewards seldom are. In accepting the challenge of a do-it-yourself marriage, you surrender all rights to convenient copouts and fifty-fifty relationships. There will be lonely times at first, and times when only your Father in Heaven can help you to determine when to compromise and when to stand firm. It would be unfair for me to promise a positive change in your partner as a result of your efforts because, remember, that's not what you're striving for; but laws have a way of fulfilling themselves, and don't be surprised at some pretty exciting results from *all* directions!

Afton J. Day serves as a Relief Society teacher in her Sandy Springs, Georgia, ward. She is the mother of three children.

When Marriages Have Problems

If we are willing to pay the price, we can turn a marital relationship into an eternal companionship—despite our differences.

By Terry R. Baker

We think we'll be different. Many of us come to marriage believing that we'll never have to resolve differences. We think our great love for each other will let us bypass the problems that "normal" couples have. For a while, differences may go unnoticed, and tolerance for each other's weaknesses and mistakes is high. This is probably good, because it gets most of us married. Without the indulgence of this early love, many of us might still be looking for some mythical Mr. or Miss Perfect. But as we begin to discover differences we didn't notice before, our visions of an eternally blissful marriage may fade.

It is unrealistic to assume we will never have marital differences. Our backgrounds, experiences, interests, expectations, and role models are usually different from our spouse's, even though on the surface they might appear similar. These differences sooner or later need to be resolved. Otherwise we might never learn to be unselfish, empathetic, and sensitive—and our marriage would suffer. So instead of cursing our differences, we should be thankful for them. But is it really possible to overcome differences and achieve unity? I've found that couples' problems seem to fall into two categories.

These two categories are disagreeing on priorities and reconciling expectations.

An example of disagreeing on priorities is the couple who comes into some unexpected money and decides to spend it on things they've needed for a long time. The husband suggests buying new tires for the car, but the wife feels the children need some new clothes. The more they talk, defending their own points of view, the more frustrated they become. They lose the excitement they had over having money to spend for the family.

Another couple might have a problem reconciling their expectations of each other. It frustrates the husband to no end that his wife can't have herself and the children ready for Sunday School on time. He hates more than most anything to walk into church late.

Such problems inevitably surface as couples balance limited resources with seemingly unlimited needs and wants, when they don't even agree on what is a need and what is a want, and they live with each other's personal habits.

Couples work through their differences at varying levels of effectiveness, with different methods. Here are the general levels, starting at the bottom and working up to a Christlike approach. These levels aren't inclusive; persons might function at one level part of the time and at different levels at other times:

Putting Each Other Down (the Worst Way)

In the world, this method is often characterized by physical fighting, swearing, and throwing things. It is accompanied by excessive selfishness, stubbornness, and the idea that "my way is the only way and I am obviously much wiser than my partner will ever be." To make sure that the other person gets this point and believes it, the partner chooses an emotional outburst designed to put the other down.

It's easy to function at this level; it takes little practice. All we need to do is to not think, be undisciplined, not read the scriptures, and ignore gospel teachings. Many characters on television and in the movies "solve" their differences this way.

Burying Feelings (a Little Better)

This method of resolving differences consists of pretending that problems don't exist. But feelings buried alive usually refuse to die. They keep surfacing, disrupting us and those close to us. Some people suffer from buried feelings for decades. Unresolved resentment, anger, disappointment, frustration, and hurt can destroy physical health and ruin marriages and families.

Functioning at this level is a small step above level one because it does require some self-control. Those practicing this technique usually adapt it from such sayings as "If you can't say something nice, don't say anything at all." This is sound advice on occasion. But when we repress important feelings, the one who feels hurt will continue to feel hurt, and the spouse will always be wondering in frustration what the problem is. This level is not recommended for those trying to create an eternal marriage.

Compromising (Better, but Not Perfect)

This level is advocated by communication specialists. It is particularly useful, they say, in solving problems of limited family resources. It is similar to the process nations use to negotiate peaceful settlements.

Couples functioning at this level usually go through a sequence of steps. First, they recognize that a conflict exists and decide to negotiate a settlement. Next, during the negotiation period, each partner recognizes the other's rights and tries to be sensitive to the other's needs. At the bargaining session, each person states what he or she would like, and then demonstrates willingness to compromise and trade. Above all, both sides try to make the settlement fair and equitable.

This level of problem-solving is popular among many couples in the world today and is a definite improvement on levels one and two. It takes work, self-control, empathy, and a desire to place the relationship on at least an equal level of importance with our own personal needs and wants. But it lacks charity.

Being Charitable (the Best Method)

This level is based on gospel principles, especially charity—the opposite of selfishness. If we have charity, we have as much love and concern for our mate as we have for ourselves. We try to understand our partner's feelings and needs; we value our relationship more than our own wants. The level and tone of voice we use in problem-solving is the same we would use if we were talking to the Savior, the prophet, or any other important person.

When Paul and Moroni defined charity (1 Corinthians 13; Moroni 7), they used such words as "suffereth long, and is kind, and envieth not, and is not puffed up, seeketh not her own, is not easily provoked, thinketh no evil, and rejoiceth not in iniquity but rejoiceth in the truth, beareth all things, believeth all things, hopeth all things, endureth all things. . . . Never faileth. . . . is the pure love of Christ, and . . . endureth forever." (Moroni 7:45-47; see also 1 Corinthians 13:4-8.) What useful counsel for husbands and wives trying to overcome differences!

These suggestions might help us use charity in solving marital problems:

a. *Deal with personal feelings first.* Intense feelings affect our self-control, which in turn influences our ability to be charitable and to communicate clearly. Therefore it is best to "cool off" first before we try to talk to our mate.

Of course, it's even better to discipline ourselves not to get upset in the first place. This is difficult for most of us, but we can do it if we undertand the nature of our emotional responses. Many of our initial feelings cannot be avoided. But if we continue to harbor these feelings, it is because we choose to.

Imagine, for example, a person functioning at level one, shouting and screaming about how terrible things are. A knock comes at the door. The transformation that takes place seems miraculous as he greets the caller in a pleasant manner. This transformation is possible because we can control such emotions if we want to.

One way to control such emotions is to stop wanting to make others look bad, to stop trying to find someone else to place the blame upon. Some find it helpful to do such things as count to ten, read poetry, play the piano, jog, or even cry. The method we choose is not important. The important thing is that we get control of our initial feelings before engaging in a serious problem-solving discussion, and that we not use our emotions in ways that are dishonest, impure, or uncharitable.

b. *Be sensitive to timing.* Some times are better for discussions than others. We may need to wait until the best time comes. It is unwise to discuss important feelings when we or our partners are tired, pressured, or hungry.

c. *Own up to the problem.* In this simple but important step, we acknowledge that we are concerned and that we aren't trying to blame the other person. Instead of saying "you make me mad when . . ." we could say something like "I have a concern that I'd like to talk to you about. Is now a good time to do it?" If the answer is yes, then continue.

d. *Begin with a sincere, positive statement related to the issue.* When we are angry, this is difficult to do—that's why we have to be in control of our feelings.

For example, the husband concerned about continually being late for church with his family should make sure that he is in control of his feelings and that his wife is also receptive. Then he might say that he is proud of how nice she and the children look when they go to church. In this way he communicates that this is not an attack and that she does not need to become defensive and counterattack.

e. *Honestly and kindly state feelings associated with this concern.* The husband might say, "I've been a little embarrassed the last few weeks when we've walked into church late." In this way we let our spouse know exactly what we've been feeling and help him or her empathize and understand our problem better.

f. *State the concern in a tentative manner rather than using absolutes.* By so doing, we acknowledge that what we are saying is only the way we see it and that our partner's views are just as important as our own. Some tentative phrases are: "I wonder if . . ."; "As I see it . . ."; "I may be wrong but . . ."; "It seems to me . . ."; "In my opinion. . . ."

g. *Be descriptive in explaining the problem. Avoid passing judgment.* It is important here to be as specific as we can in describing the other person's behavior, rather than making judgments such as "You don't even care if we are late or not." For example, I could say: "As I remember it, the last three Sundays three of the children were still in bed at 9:00. That gives them only an hour to wash, eat, get ready, and travel to church. That doesn't appear to me to be enough time."

After we are sure our partner understands both our feelings and our perception of facts about the problems, and after we have given our spouse a chance to state his or her own feelings and perceptions of the facts, then it is time to move on to the resolution step. Unfortunately, too many of us try to skip all of the above steps and just blurt out such things as "What are you going to do about always making us late for church?" This type of attack is dishonest—it nearly always makes the situation worse.

h. *Make some suggestions, stating what you are willing to do to help accomplish those suggestions.* This shows that you are not just a complainer but are willing to help make changes. The husband might offer to plan his Sunday mornings so that he can help get the younger children ready. He might add, "Is there anything else I can do to help?"

i. *Be flexible.* If your suggestions are not acceptable, be willing to accommodate your mate's perceptions of how the problem can best be resolved.

For some, charity problem-solving suggestions are natural and easy. Others find them more difficult. The prophet Joseph Smith taught that no man has ever reached perfection in a moment, and that perfection is a step-by-step process. (See *Teachings of the Prophet Joseph Smith*, p. 51.) The important thing is remembering that we are on a charted course, continually improving, accepting our failures as new starting points, and never giving up.

If we are willing to pay this price, if we are optimistic, we can turn a mortal marital relationship into an eternal companionship—despite our differences.

Terry R. Baker, father of eight children, works in the Church Educational System as regional coordinator for the Houston, Texas, area. He is currently serving as the Friendswood, Texas, Stake clerk.

Breaking the Cycle

A case study of conflict in marriage.

By C. Ross Clement

Some time ago, David and Ellen came to my office seeking help for their marriage. Their relationship was basically a good one—they felt a great commitment to each other. But they were finding it increasingly difficult to communicate without contention, and they wanted to learn how to work together to solve their problems. They began with an incident that had occurred a few nights earlier. David had arrived home late from work. Ellen was upset.

"You knew I had an art class at 7:30," she said.

"Sorry, honey, but I just had to work late."

"Didn't want me to go and leave you with the kids, did you?"

"No, that's not it at all. I had a lot to do to get ready for inventory. You know how important that is."

"That's all you seem to care about. Why should your job always come before me and the kids?"

"I'm just trying to provide for the family. Sometimes that takes more time than you realize. Besides, your place is at home, not at some art class. I don't like the idea of your going back to school so you can get a job. If you'd just let me work at it, I could make enough money to support us."

According to David and Ellen, this confrontation was

similar to many others they'd had. They always repeated the same general pattern of communication: one accusation led to another, and the original point of contention was soon lost in a storm of spiraling debate and criticism—where past mistakes were recalled. Nothing was ever resolved.

Anyone who has been trapped in a vicious cycle of conflict knows the accompanying feeling of helplessness and hopelessness. But David and Ellen found their way out. The following principles proved helpful to them. I believe the principles could benefit most marriages.

1. *Be teachable.* Paradoxically, those who need, want, and even seek help are sometimes unwilling to accept it when it is given. Efforts to solve marital problems are unsuccessful when partners refuse to be teachable or to change when change is necessary. Problems will remain unsolved if either the husband or the wife pretends to go through the motion of solving problems but is intent upon influencing or manipulating the other partner into doing all the changing.

Before proceeding any further, David and Ellen, for example, agreed to fast and pray for the Spirit of the Lord to be with them. They recognized a great need for divine intervention, and prayed that the Lord would touch their hearts. They also prayed for purity of purpose and for a willingness to share and learn from one another.

2. *Use sound relationship principles revealed by the Lord.* One of the Lord's standards for relationships between his children is given in D&C 121:41-42: "No power or influence can or ought to be maintained . . . [except] by persuasion, by long-suffering, by gentleness and meekness, and by love unfeigned; By kindness, and pure knowledge." If a couple wants their problem-solving efforts to be effective, they must strive to incorporate these qualities in their marital relationships. They must pray for the Lord's help in learning to treat each other in Christlike ways.

The Lord also warns against those who would "exercise control or dominion or compulsion upon the souls of the children of men." Not only is "the Spirit of the Lord . . . grieved" (see D&C 121:37), but marital relationships suffer.

One common mistake couples in conflict often make is to

judge the intents and actions of one another. It is a mistake for couples to speak for each other, as if they possessed the ability to read thoughts: "You've never really considered my needs. All you're interested in is your job." "You don't care at all about my work. You don't appreciate what I do for you."

These kinds of statements are easily identified by the overuse of the word *you*, and are sometimes referred to as "you messages." "You messages" put others on the defensive by placing blame upon them. But when we follow the Lord's principles for good relationships, we concentrate on improving ourselves before attempting to encourage others to change their behavior.

3. *Strive to fully understand your partner's point of view.* Most couples enter marriage with a preconceived notion of what a husband or wife ought to be like. Problems arise when each has a different view on the matter, or when either or both views are not in harmony with the will of the Lord for how we should conduct our lives.

Ellen thought a good husband ought to be home more of the time; David believed he was fulfilling his responsibility best by reaching financial success, no matter how much time it required. David thought that a good wife ought to be content to stay home and take care of the children; Ellen believed she ought to go to school and help support the family. The reasons for these divergent views can be seen in the background experiences each brought to the marriage.

Because his own family had been very poor, David felt compelled to become financially independent. Relentlessly, he had striven to rise within the management levels of the company he worked for, and to invest in stocks and real estate. He was just beginning to realize the financial benefits of his extensive commitments. To him, the idea of cutting back on the job was equivalent to failure.

Ellen was reared in a home where both parents were employed and shared in domestic responsibilities. Both were college graduates and encouraged each of their children to obtain degrees. After marriage and the birth of her first child, Ellen had dropped out of school. But she had retained a strong desire to graduate. To abandon her desire to go back to college would have meant giving up some of the ideals that had meant so much to her family and been part of her background.

An important part of the communication process must be an understanding of your own as well as your partner's expectations in marriage. With such an understanding, the change process can be much easier.

4. *Fully and sensitively share your view of the problem.* When marital problems occur, some husbands and wives share so little information about their feelings that the partner is unable to understand the problem. Instead of clearly sharing their own perspective, some people pout, displace angry feelings (slam the door or bang pots and pans in the sink), downplay the problem ("Nothing's bothering me") or give insufficient information ("I'd like to crawl in a hole and stay there. I'm so unhappy"). Sometimes, to avoid facing the issues involved or to avoid personal responsibility, the individual may attack and blame the spouse.

The Apostle Paul said, "Except ye utter by the tongue words easy to be understood, how shall it be known what is spoken?" (1 Corinthians 14:9.)

When helping couples share a problem, I encourage appropriate disclosure so that marital partners may understand one another. Appropriate disclosure leads to better understanding; inappropriate disclosure may offend, accuse, or wound.

There is an important difference between clearly and sensitively disclosing one's experience and saying anything and everything that comes to mind as a means of venting feelings. Couples who "let it all hang out" usually end up hurting each other and destroying a relationship. Where there are angry feelings, couples should look for underlying causes (which usually include unmet needs or some kind of painful experience). By focusing upon the underlying problem and resolving it, one can defuse angry feelings. The ideas that follow will help couples get at the core of most relationship issues and problems, while avoiding the temptation to dwell on secondary angry feelings. Information to be disclosed includes:

- What we see, hear, or otherwise observe through our senses. (This is pure sensory data, which a television camera or microphone would record; *not* information that has been distorted by feelings, such as, "I can see from the look on your face that you don't love me anymore.")

David more accurately reported his observations this way: "Ellen, when I came home from work last night and entered the door, it seemed to me that you turned your back on me, set the utensils on the table, and walked away. You only spoke to me once during dinner—when I tried to talk things out with you. Then you said I cared more for my job than for you."

• How we process or interpret the information received: "From your actions I felt you were angry at me. I felt you avoided me for the rest of the evening. I felt your actions were unjust."

• The resulting feelings: "Whenever I see you respond to me that way, it hurts. I begin to wonder if it's really worth it. It seems like I end up feeling like a failure no matter what I do."

• What we'd sincerely like to do about a given situation: "When I arrived home, I wanted to apologize to you for being late, and yet I didn't want to because I felt you were being unfair to me. (This includes the interpretation.) The reason I work hard is to be able to provide you and the kids with a good standard of living. And yet, I want to be fair and better understand your point of view."

• What we are actually willing to *commit* ourselves to do: "Let me hear what you have to say about the situation." After David had disclosed himself in this non-accusing, sensitive way, there was little question in Ellen's mind as to his immediate perception of the problem.

5. *Seek a shared understanding.* When a husband or wife shares a problem, the most typical response of the partner is to defend himself (justifying his actions) or to counterattack (blaming the partner for the problem just shared). Couples who argue seldom listen to each other. While one is talking, the other is busy formulating his counter-argument. Instead of lashing back, Ellen sought to better understand her husband's thoughts, feelings, and intentions. This was done by:

• Expressing her intention to understand: "I'd like to make sure I understand what you're saying." Or, "Let me see if I heard you right."

• Summarizing in her own words the message she heard, asking for confirmation of her understanding: "You're saying that you really do care for me and that you work long hours to help make sure the children and I will be well cared for. Is that right?"

Other approaches that invite helpful disclosure include:

• Asking open-ended questions: "Can you tell me more about what you're feeling?"

• Reflecting feelings: "You feel hurt when you believe I've unjustly accused you."

• Checking out your perception of what is being said: "The tone of your voice and the expression of your face tell me that you're angry, too. Is that right?"

After listening carefully to her husband until she understood his feelings, Ellen began to disclose her own thoughts, feelings, and intentions concerning the problem (see step 4). David refrained from counter-arguing using instead the understanding skills (step 5) to invite full disclosure from his wife.

Since their problems and misunderstandings were complex, David and Ellen spent several hours discussing them over the ensuing weeks. Because they were learning to communicate in a new way, there were times when they found it easy to slip back into old habits of blaming, criticizing, and refusing to share true feelings. Recognizing the need to solve the problem, however, they persistently refocused their attention on the communication skills being learned, and they gradually became adept at the process and responsive to each other. Also, each came to understand and appreciate the viewpoint of his partner.

6. *Seek solutions to the problem.* After obtaining a shared understanding, Ellen and David then went to the next and important step of generating possible solutions. They did this, first, by identifying Church guidelines and scriptural counsel related to their challenges.

Then they brainstormed several possibilities. They wrote down every idea that came up, without criticizing each other's suggestions: "You could quit your job and find another one that only requires forty hours a week." "You could give up your idea of going back to school." "I could find someone to trade babysitting with so I could have a night to do as I want." "I could re-evaluate my work situation. Maybe by delegating more, I could spend more time at home."

Finally, they evaluated each suggestion. After writing down as many suggestions as possible, they proceeded to evaluate each suggestion, fully disclosing feelings, thoughts, and intentions, while seeking a shared understanding of each other's viewpoint:

"I really love my job. I believe it offers the potential for growth and financial success. However, I love you and the children even more. I'd prefer not to sacrifice the job unless I have to, and I really don't believe I do. I'd like to scratch the suggestion of quitting my job and consider re-evaluating my work situation and making whatever adjustments need to be made."

"I don't want to give up the idea of going back to school. Not only do I like a break, but, to me, an education is a measure of security. If anything were ever to happen to you, I'd like to have some marketable skills in case I had to go to work. I'd still like to take a class if possible."

David and Ellen proceeded through each suggestion, alternately sharing and listening to the feelings of each other. There was no attempt to persuade or manipulate each other into a particular selection. They evaluated their ideas in light of gospel standards and Church counsel and then made their decision a matter of prayer. Eventually they worked out a solution that was mutually acceptable and in harmony with the Lord's will.

David agreed to talk to his employer about his need to cut down on long hours. To his surprise, he found that his boss was also somewhat concerned about his long hours at work and the possible strains it placed upon his family. He assured David that his value as an employee could even increase if he learned to delegate a little more. David experienced a change in attitude toward his job and family. And because there was less conflict at home, he found that he could concentrate more on his job responsibilities while at work.

Ellen agreed to be more responsive to her husband and children. She also arranged to begin an evening class at a local university. With the additional support of her husband, she noticed that her feelings toward her domestic responsibilities dramatically improved, and she found it easier to be loving and giving.

The couple faced additional challenges in life. But their improved ability to communicate with each other enabled them to work more effectively toward finding solutions. They felt that the Lord was blessing them for their efforts—and they found greater peace and satisfaction in their marriage.

As you strive to improve your way of communicating in marriage, these steps may seem awkward at first. Like most new skills, they require practice before they will come naturally. But I've seen these steps work over and over again, particularly when the individuals invite the Lord to help them and when they are sincere and willing to share responsibility for the causes and solutions to marriage problems.

C. Ross Clement is employed as a training and development specialist at Brigham Young University for LDS Social Services. He is bishop of the South Jordan Seventh Ward.

MANAGING MONEY

The Dangers of Debt in Marriage

It is not at our material possessions that debt strikes, but at our spiritual treasures.

By Rulon T. Burton

It was a fresh and invigorating spring morning when Dale and Gloria (the names of all couples mentioned in this article have been changed) came to my office to see me. Their primary purpose for making a nine-hundred-mile journey from their home in another state was to bring a sizable sum of money. We shook hands, glad to see each other after such a long time. It had been a full ten years since they moved, leaving behind a virtual mountain of unpaid bills, legal entanglements, and unfulfilled obligations. Since then they had worked hard together saving their money. Dale handed me a check for more than $12,000 and asked me to locate and satisfy their former creditors.

"This has really been a good experience for us," Gloria said. "Believe me, we've come a long way since you saw us last!"

"But," Dale hastened to add, "we never want to go through this again!"

Dale and Gloria's story is not unusual in my experience. As an attorney specializing in bankruptcy reorganizations, I have seen it repeated many times—usually without the happy ending. Many years ago, when their family was young and they were both struggling to make ends meet, Dale made a series of unwise financial commitments. The end result was insurmountable debt.

It is important to know the dangers of debt. Experience has shown me that uncontrolled debt results not just in the loss of money or material goods; it can also seriously try the bonds of marriage and cause much disunity within the family.

For Dale and Gloria, the loving bonds of marriage had been tried and tested through their ordeal. Before they came to see me, they had gone through many tears and much anguish. Months stretched into years in which there were many heated discussions over money—what should have been done, what shouldn't have been done. The pleasing part of their story is that in the end they put themselves to work in the same harness where together they slowly but steadily pulled themselves out of their problem.

When I was a boy, I used to watch my Uncle Frank "pull horses" at the state fair. It was apparent that winning depended not just on the strength of the horses, but also on their ability to use that strength as a team, working together. I have seen the leather break and the harness gouge into the flesh of the horses when they were not pulling together. Marriage is like that. It is two people teamed together with a bond of love, facing life's challenges in harmony with each other. Pulling together makes the job relatively light. But heavy debt not only increases the burden they must bear, it also wears away the love and affection and mutual care that makes it possible for them to work as a team.

Perhaps we cannot always avoid debt. Without it, purchasing a home would be nearly impossible for most people; buying a car would be very difficult; and for many, an education would be out of reach without a loan. In these three instances, a debt is justifiable in helping a family achieve its goals. But going into debt to purchase ordinary consumer goods is a very risky thing—that is, the benefits are extremely limited, considering the price a family may eventually have to pay. My personal opinion is that we can and should avoid consumer debt altogether.

But why should we avoid using consumer credit? After all, our society promotes the use of credit, of buying things "on time," of obtaining the use of items before we have fully paid for them. In fact, the use of debt is supposed to make our environment more affluent. Credit stimulates the economy. It makes more goods available to us. If we are careful, why shouldn't we use credit for more than just our home or car? Perhaps the story of Boyd and Connie, a young couple who finally came to me for legal advice, will illustrate the dangers of consumer debt.

Boyd and Connie were a happily married couple. Both were working at well-paying jobs. The mortgage on their home was not large compared to their combined salaries, so they did not worry about incurring small debts here and there through the use of credit cards. With the security of their two jobs, they also bought furniture on installment payments, clothing on a thirty-day account, and two cars that required monthly payments. They were satisfied. They were able to meet all their payments, and they enjoyed the things they were purchasing while they were paying for them. In fact, buying on credit worked so well for them, that they escalated their debts by borrowing money (through a second mortgage) to pay for a good Christmas, a "needed vacation," and for some home improvements.

With the steady incomes of their permanent jobs, Boyd and Connie felt secure in their early affluence. But circumstances changed for them. They had wanted a family for some time, and when Connie left work to have her first baby, they began to realize just how dependent they really were on both of their incomes. When the baby was born, Connie hastened back to work after only a two-month leave of absence. It was a special strain for her. She truly wanted to be with her infant but now felt compelled to continue working to pay for the things which before had seemed so important.

Events worsened when Boyd suddenly found himself out of work. He was shocked and disillusioned that his "permanent" job had suddenly turned into unemployment. For several months the couple struggled along on Connie's income alone. In the meantime, their creditors were very busy trying to collect their money. Boyd and Connie, having no answers to give their creditors, avoided their calls and contacts. Boyd was soon reemployed but at a lesser income. They still could not see their way out of their debt problems.

Debt had made Boyd and Connie vulnerable (as it does

anyone who chooses to use credit), so that when emergencies came they were unable to handle them. Certainly they could have taken precautions. They could have bought less, or they could have saved money for the arrival of their baby. Yes, they could have made better decisions. But even in relatively "safe" dealings with debt, we leave ourselves open to the unexpected. Unemployment, illness, hospitalization, pregnancy, or just poor judgment on financial matters can all upset the smooth flow of required installment payments. And once a payment is missed, problems seem to compound and escalate. Harassment from creditors, repossession of the goods bought on credit, lawsuits, tax penalties, and even the loss of a home can all result.

Because so many circumstances are largely beyond our control, debt is *always* risky business. Whenever consumer credit is used, it compounds our vulnerability to the adverse effects of any change in the regular pattern of our lives—just as it did with Boyd and Connie. On the other hand, the less debt we get into, the more independent we are of circumstances. This is why I believe we should restrict our "necessary debt" to the home mortgage, to the automobile (with judicious restraint), and to modest debt when necessary to obtain an education.

Our Church leaders have consistently admonished us to avoid unnecessary debt. In the April 1975 general conference, President Spencer W. Kimball said, "All my life from childhood I have heard the Brethren saying, 'get out of debt and stay out of debt.' " (In Conference Report, April 1975, p. 166.) And Elder John H. Vandenberg, when he was Presiding Bishop of the Church, stated the following:

"Unwarrantable indebtedness is one of the curses of this day and age. It causes many people to live their lives in bondage. The lure of buying on time under the 'easy payment plan' too often puts a millstone around the neck of the purchaser; and when once in the credit rut, it is very hard to get out. . . .

"When a family finds itself too far in debt," he continued, "the atmosphere of discouragement enters the home, relationships become tense, tempers become short, and marital troubles begin to erupt. To meet the indebtedness, the mother may frequently leave her children to themselves while she finds employment out of the home. Irregularities in the home follow:

service to God is disregarded, tithing is neglected, prayers become less frequent, persons begin to feel separated and apart from God and church." (In Conference Report, Oct. 1966, p. 66.)

This is just what happened to Boyd and Connie. Their financial situation was at the crisis stage: a mountain of debt, and not enough income to overcome it. Having no solutions, they began to turn alternately against each other and then against their creditors. Connie later told me:

"Our relationship got to the point where Boyd and I separated for a while. After he lost his job, one of the creditors called me at my work and asked if I knew where Boyd was living. I told them quite honestly that I did not. They said they were going to find out. The next day they called my mother-in-law in California, who didn't even know we were having troubles. They told her that Boyd was not working at his job and that since he and I were separated, they wanted to know from her where he was living so they could collect their account."

Connie went on: "People collecting for creditors have called at home and left messages with my children and the babysitters and have caused us considerable embarrassment. At one point, the children asked me, 'Mom, are we really poor?' "

I met this couple in the midst of their crisis. In moments of weakness and stress, Connie had angrily accused her husband of not fulfilling his role as breadwinner. Boyd, in turn, had accused her of being worldly in wanting the clothes, furniture, and luxuries that had gotten them into their mess. Their accusations against each other contained both truths and untruths, mostly half-truths. Their marriage was slipping; their children seemed to be neglected.

I was able to help them straighten out their finances, but what about their marriage? What of all the bad feelings that had come between them? They could work their way out of debt, but how would they repair the damage done to an eternal bond? It would take time, effort, and love.

Through many such experiences, I have discovered a great truth: debt leaves more scars on *people* than on pocketbooks. It is not at our material possessions that debt strikes its most painful blow, but at our spiritual treasures. Far worse than any loss of money or property is the damage done to a marriage because of debt. I have worked with hundreds of couples who have become victimized by debt. In all of these case histories there is a sad and strikingly clear pattern: financial troubles produce marital problems.

Couples who face financial trials are typically immersed in the perplexities and uncertainties of not knowing how to solve their problems. Then comes a panicky sense of helplessness, a sense of being alone in a world where everyone is somehow against them. Eventually, the strain often turns them against each other.

It is tragic that couples caught in heavy debt so often draw apart at the very time when they need each other's support the most. But this need not and should not be. It is when couples choose to love and forgive and squarely face their problems *together*, rather than argue and despair, that one recognizes the great strength of two people working in harmony with a bond of love.

On one occasion I had the sweet experience of seeing a wife quietly place her hand on her husband's, look into his eyes, and earnestly confirm that she had forgiven him of gross financial errors—errors that had caused them five years of stress and strain, near poverty, and much grief before the problems were surmounted. There were no recriminations, no accusations, and no "false forgiving" of her husband's past mistakes. She had shared in those mistakes, at least in some degree. From that day forward they would work together as a team. Together they solved and overcame a huge problem in their lives.

This happy ending was not the result of chance. The reason they were able to overcome their financial and marital difficulties was that somewhere in the midst of things, they came to a turning point. I call this the "moment of truth." It is when a husband and wife are both willing to take responsibility for their mistakes. It is when they are willing to *resolve* problems rather than to fix blame. It is when a husband and wife quit working against each other and start working together again.

It is at this time that a testimony that comes from dedicated living of the gospel becomes a strong support. A gospel-oriented marriage helps a couple adopt the healthy attitude that says, "I have done wrong and I have made mistakes, but I forgive myself, and from this day forward I will take whatever steps are necessary to solve this problem. I place no blame; I point no finger at my spouse or at my creditors. I have love in my heart for my fellowmen and a great appreciation and gratitude for my Father in Heaven, who gives me the strength and the opportunity to go forward."

In the gospel we find the admonition to love. An ability to love one's partner and to forgive, forget, and overlook what appear to be weaknesses can be the saving balm to prevent or heal marital anxieties. It is through the miracle of love and working together that a marriage can weather any financial storm.

By following our Church leaders' advice, by using great caution whenever contemplating going into debt, and by preparing against unexpected changes in circumstances, a husband and wife can secure themselves against the woes of indebtedness. But if debt is already present, if it threatens to damage the eternal bond of marriage, there is a solution. It involves accepting responsibility and forgiving the weaknesses in others. But mostly, it involves love.

Husbands and wives who strive to keep the first and second great commandments—to love the Lord their God with all their might, mind, and strength, and their neighbor as themselves (see Matthew 22:36-40)—are the ones who are prepared against the dangers of debt and can feel truly secure about the treasure that no creditor can repossess: the treasure of everlasting marriage.

Rulon T. Burton, a lawyer specializing in bankruptcy cases, and father of three children, is the Gospel Doctrine teacher in the Granite Third Ward.

Family Finances

How a couple handles money can make or mar their marriage.

By Orson Scott Card

For many couples, handling money comes easily; but for others, conflicts over finances can sometimes seem insurmountable. Among many other things, a new marriage is very much like a corporate merger. Two people, possibly with very different habits in handling money, suddenly find themselves trying to combine those different methods with one source of funds and one household to take care of.

After interviewing dozens of Latter-day Saint couples from Florida to Michigan, from Washington, D.C., to the San Francisco Bay area, I reached one simple conclusion; no one way of handling money is always best. Even though my sampling is limited to the United States, the general conclusions can apply to Saints everywhere.

Among some couples the husband handled all the money, wrote all the checks, and gave the wife an allowance for household expenses. On the average they were neither more nor less content with their approach than the couples in which the wife wrote all the checks and the husband arranged to have a spending-money allowance. In between those extremes were dozens of couples who had separate checking accounts, or who discussed and paid the bills together, or who took turns handling the finances. And there didn't seem to be any significant difference between couples who had very little money or who had a great deal: there were as many who had financial problems with a lot of money as with a very little.

What *does* make the difference, then, between couples who can handle finances with ease and those who can't? Couples who handled their finances successfully seemed to have several things in common: communication between spouses, reasonable expectations, willingness to budget, and rejection of debt.

Communication between Spouses

If both husband and wife know what is going on with the money, it doesn't matter who is actually writing the checks. But when either the husband or wife feels unsure—insecure—about where the money is going, problems begin to arise.

Kent and Teresa Barker, a young couple in Sterling Park, Virginia, liked the way Kent's parents handled the money. "My mother always wrote out the checks and kept track of them. Dad would just go over the checkbook with her and see that things were getting taken care of for the month. That's the way we handle it, and every month we jointly compare what we've spent with our budget and see how we've come out. Neither of us has to ask the other for money—we both know exactly where we stand financially, how much we can or can't afford for special things."

Brother and Sister Earl Roueche of McLean, Virginia, have followed a similar procedure through many years of marriage. "I don't think either one of us ever spends any money without the other one knowing what it's being spent for. We talk over even the minor decisions. After all, minor purchases add up fast! Whether we're spending more money for food, buying clothes, or deciding on whether to buy a car, we always discuss in some detail before we do it. Many things we discuss with our children, because it will affect them, too. We wanted to buy a piano one year. We took several of the children with us, and then after we had looked at several pianos we told the salesman that we would come back later after a family discussion. He really laughed when we came back, because he had thought we were just making an excuse for not buying a piano! But after talking it over, we decided *as a family* that we could buy it—though it meant cutting out some other extras. The children didn't mind, because they felt it was *their* decision, too."

That seems to be the important thing, whether all those involved feel like the decision is mutual. The problems seem to come when one spouse or the other starts to decide arbitrarily. "No, you can't buy that" can be frustrating when one spouse is always saying it to the other.

"I had never been involved with the finances," one woman said. "My husband made all the decisions, and I never knew what was going on. So imagine my surprise when all of a sudden I found out we were on the verge of bankruptcy!" In this case, the husband had simply believed that men were supposed to handle the money. He wasn't very good at it, though, and his wife was! So they decided that she would balance the books; they began discussing every purchase, every payment, and deciding together—and with their combined wisdom and mutual self-restraint they were able to avoid bankruptcy after all.

"One thing that never works," say the Kay Christensens of Kansas City, Missouri, "is the attitude, 'This is *my* money, so I'll go spend it the way I like.' No matter whether the husband or wife is bringing in the money, all the money should belong equally to both. Neither the husband nor the wife has the right to go spending 'because it belongs to me.'"

Several families found that communicating about money had another good effect. "She is a good financial conscience," one husband said. "When I'm tempted to let something go in order to buy something else, it helps me to keep control when I know that my wife will worry about the payment I didn't make." And discussing before buying is a good way to avoid "impulse shopping." "We never buy things on a whim," many couples told me. "We always discuss. And that means that usually we don't waste our money on anything foolish."

Talking things over between husband and wife is not a guarantee that nothing bad will ever happen financially. But it *is* a guarantee that one spouse or the other won't be shocked when something goes wrong, won't be resentful when belt-tightening is needed, won't fritter away the family's financial resources.

And when both spouses have agreed on the way the money should be spent, there can be few quarrels over what "you" did with the money.

Reasonable Expectations

"One of my sons had a terrible time with money when he first got married," one father told me. "His wife had been raised in a wealthy family, and she was used to getting what she wanted. The trouble was that my son was going to college and holding down a part-time job, and there just wasn't any money. But she would decide they had to have an electric can opener because her parents had had one, and she wheedled until he bought her one. That kind of thing happened again and again, until they were in pretty bad financial shape."

Sometimes one spouse or the other—or both—hasn't really learned the value of money. Accustomed to having money whenever they want it, accustomed to all the luxuries of their parents' homes, they don't realize that the early years of marriage almost always require sacrifices. The husband may be going to school, but even if his education is essentially complete, he won't reach his earning peak for many years. The beautiful home with lovely furnishings doesn't come right away in most cases.

Husbands' expectations can cause problems, too. "I was single for many years before I married," said one man. "I was used to buying whatever I wanted. You just can't do that anymore when the children start coming. We were deeply in debt before I finally learned that lesson. The boat would have to wait a few years!"

Indeed, a bishop in the South said, "Time and time again I talk to families who don't have enough money to pay tithing, to meet basic food needs—but they're families who last month bought a boat! There are people in our ward who take their minds off their financial troubles by going out to dinner and a movie every weekend! When their son's Little League team goes to tournament, they go too and stay in an expensive motel and eat at restaurants. They fritter away their money and then wonder where it went.

"People like that," he went on, "need to take a hard look at what their income actually is. They have to stop expecting their money to buy what their wealthier neighbors' money buys. Even if you do catch up with the Joneses, there will always be the Smiths with even more, and now you have to keep up with them. I wish there was some way to convince people to just keep up with themselves and forget the neighbors' life-style!"

Richard and Kathy Halvorsen of Overland Park, Kansas, found where their priorities belonged. "We like nice things, and now we have some nice things, but neither of us has ever gotten completely depressed because we could not have a certain luxury. What we can afford to buy is a necessity! We were dirt poor when we were first married and went to school on a shoestring," Brother Halvorsen reported. "Kathy worked me through college—and got her own degree at the same time. We learned how to do without things. Now when we can afford something, it is a pleasant surprise."

Willingness to Budget

"We sit down and figure out all our basic needs: tithing, food, clothing, house payments, utilities—that kind of thing," said Rulon Munns of Lakeland, Florida. "Then we make a list of things we want or feel we need, like a new car or a couch or a dining room set, and list them in their order of importance. After we have paid all the necessary bills, we start saving the rest of the money for the number one thing on our list. After we've bought that, we go to number two." That seems to be the key to many families' financial contentment: budgeting the necessities first, and then using the leftover money—if there is any—wisely.

"What surprised us when we started to budget," one Salt Lake City couple confessed ruefully, "was that we actually had more necessary payments than we had income! And here we'd been spending as if we had extra money every month. It took careful ordering of priorities and skimping for quite a while to get on top of things. Sticking to that budget was hard at first. But when we compare our financial situation then to the way it is now, we know we'll never stop budgeting."

A young lawyer who is in his fifth year with a major law firm said, "All of the other associates own large homes. When we were looking for a house we wanted one of those big homes so badly. We debated over it—we could have got a loan to buy one of those big homes, but our payments would have been so large we would have been scraping to buy food and clothes and to pay the utilities. And so we bought this much smaller home, and now we have money left over to *live* on."

Before going into any major purchase, most of the better money-managing couples drew up a year's budget in advance, figuring exactly what the large payments would do to the rest of their finances. "Budgeting keeps your eyes open," said Carlos M. Bowman of Midland, Michigan.

The Bert Ray Wanlasses of Detroit, Michigan, could have bought some furniture a year after they bought their first home. The payments seemed low—but then they drew up the budget. "We realized that if we bought the furniture, something else essential, like our tithing, would have to be neglected. So we paid tithing and bought slipcovers. We lived with those slipcovers for five or six years. We eventually paid cash for the furniture."

An important part of budgeting is writing down where the money actually goes. "Once after we listed all the budgeted things—house, car, insurance, food—we thought we could save about two hundred dollars," say the Deane M. Gearigs of Roseville, Michigan. "But by the end of the month, there was maybe five dollars left. Where did it go?" They kept careful track of it and realized that the money was going for important things that couldn't be changed. "We changed the budget to include those expenses, and now there's no unconscious flow of money that we're not aware of—those 'extras' are figured as part of the budget."

For a budget to work, it's essential that a couple know what *all* their needs really are—not just the major payments. One Salt Lake City man confessed, "It used to bother me that my wife kept asking for more and more money for household expenses. But then I realized that I understood no more about grocery prices than *she* understood about the expenses of taking care of the car. So now we keep each other posted on what prices are doing, what the needs are, and figure it right into our budget."

And one bishop said, "When my financial clerk moved away, it was about a month before I could get a new one. I kept the ward's books for that month and discovered that the

Church has an ideal system for keeping track of which account the money is going into. So I set up our family accounts using the Church's accounting system. It works perfectly—I always know exactly where our money's going and where it's gone."

A budget is no guarantee that there won't be problems—medical expenses, unexpected property assessments, a steep rise in insurance rates, a sudden family emergency. All were cited as reasons why a good budget is occasionally broken. But without a budget, many families live in a state of perpetual emergency, never sure why there isn't enough money to pay the bills. With a plan that is carefully followed, a family can at least have the security of knowing exactly where they stand financially.

Rejection of Debt for Most Purchases

"I worked full time at the Forest Service while I was a full-time student getting my degree," said Bishop Jack Green of Sterling Park, Virginia. "And he was married," his wife added. Yet when he finished his education they were in a better financial situation than when they married. How? They were careful. And they refused to go into debt.

"When we moved into our first unfurnished house we decided we were going to furnish it for $200. The house had a stove and that was all. We bought a secondhand refrigerator, an inexpensive dinette set, a used couch and chair, a used vacuum cleaner, a cheap new mattress, and used bedsprings—and we kept it under two hundred! We still have that couch downstairs. It's pretty beat up, but it's useable."

Many successful couples insisted on one point: "We didn't run out and buy a house like our parent's house and furnish it like that. There's only one way that can be done—excessive debt. And we refused to go into debt for furnishings at that point in our marriage."

In two areas most families did go into debt: for the house and the car. A few families rejected debt even on the car, though I met no one who had paid cash for a house.

But other debts? Jay Foster Irwin of Detroit, Michigan, says, "We have charge cards for convenience, but whenever possible we pay by check. And we try not to let the bills from credit cards pile up for more than a month."

Robert Laird, a bishop in Orem, Utah, counsels young couples not only to tithe, but also to save. "Even if it's only ten dollars a month, it adds up. And saving gives you a cushion. With money in the bank, you aren't as tempted to go into debt." The eventual goal? "Have enough set aside to handle emergencies. After that you save for other purchases." Anyone who has ever had his car's automatic transmission break down knows that a few hundred dollars in the bank is vital.

Many couples found that the temptation to go into debt became strong when they got their first good job. "When we realized that we now had all that money coming in every month," one husband said, "we began to think that twenty-five dollars a month here and thirty dollars a month there wasn't very much at all. But we caught ourselves in time. When we save money in order to pay cash for something, the bank pays us interest while we wait. But when we go into debt to buy something, *we* pay interest. It makes no sense. Besides, when we've finished paying for something we buy on time, it's already old. But when we pay cash for something, we own it completely when it's brand new!"

Another problem is the automatic raise. "I knew a raise was coming in February, so I didn't worry," one young man said. "When the raise came, I was already behind." The solution? "Now we don't spend money until it's in the bank. There's nothing we need so badly we can't wait for it except food, necessary clothing, and shelter."

Sometimes, however, debt is justifiable. Carolyn Green of Sterling Park, Virginia, wanted a piano, but they couldn't afford it. She and her husband figured out that if she taught a few piano students she could pay for the instrument in three years. "Even so, we saved up the first year's payments in advance, just in case. Then we bought the piano and made the payments out of my piano lesson money. We would never have gone into debt for a piano if we hadn't been sure it could pay for itself. Now I just teach my own children to play, but the money we save on their piano lessons makes it a good investment!"

As any accountant can tell you, debt is sometimes a legitimate tool of finance—when it comes to investments. When the item to be purchased is going to pay for itself, like the Greens' piano or a van for a sign painter or a typewriter for a freelance secretary, borrowing can be essential. But since the debt must still be repaid even if the money-making project doesn't work out well, it is wise to invest in items that retain value, so that they can be resold if that becomes necessary. Debt can also be legitimately used for capital investments, such as land or buildings or businesses. (However, borrowing money in order to speculate can easily lead to serious difficulty and is contrary to the counsel of Church leaders.)

Buying something on credit is also sometimes not only legitimate but necessary in order to establish a good credit rating. The kind of debt that most finance-wise couples seem to avoid is borrowing to pay for things that do *not* retain value, things that do *not* "pay for themselves"—like furniture, vacations, minor purchases, household appliances, clothing, food storage, and such "pleasure items" as stereos, radios, expensive sets of books, and art objects. As one couple that lives comfortably on a modest income pointed out, "We can't enjoy using something that we don't own—and we don't feel like we own something until it's completely paid for. So we figure, if we can't pay cash, we can't afford it."

Money Has Never Been a Problem

A young couple in Provo, Utah, struggling through college with three children on only three thousand dollars a year, told me: "Money has never been a problem with us. How could it? We don't have any!" But speaking seriously, they said, "We refuse to quarrel over money. We are determined to be happy. Why be miserable because we live in a cramped apartment? It just makes us closer!"

And that seems to be the biggest difference of all between the couples who handle money easily and those who suffer over it. Time after time the couples who, no matter how large or small their income, had a harmonious relationship over finances said, "We don't really care that much about owning things. It's nice—but we can do without it. What's important is each other." With that attitude the obstacles are rarely insurmountable. Even when financial problems do come, the couple can face them in unity, refusing to be divided by difficulty. The experiences of Latter-day Saint families I interviewed points to several principles of handling money:

1. Communicate! One spouse should never be unsure of what is going on with the finances. All but the most trivial decisions should be made together combining the wisdom of both husband and wife.

2. Expect only what is reasonable. Money doesn't come easily, especially early in marriage. Neither husband nor wife should expect to be able to spend as they did when they were single.

3. Budget! Plan ahead and follow the plan as closely as you can. Record where the money went. Unless you know where you really want the money to go, it won't go there! But be prepared to adjust the budget to meet emergency and unplanned needs.

4. For most purchases, reject debt! The temptation to buy now and pay later must generally be avoided if a couple hopes to be financially secure. Do not borrow to invest in speculative ventures.

5. Remember that your marriage is more important than anything you might own, more important than any problem you might face. Don't let money be a wedge between you.

"We have enough," they said. *Enough* ranged from a tiny basement with two beds for four children to a seven-bedroom house with a view of the sea. For many, enough is not an amount—it is an attitude. And if a family is content to live on what they can earn, and no more, then they will almost always have enough. Enough, at least, to be happy.

Orson Scott Card, a freelance writer and journalist, serves as a high councilor in his Greensboro, North Carolina, stake.

LOVING AN INACTIVE OR NONMEMBER SPOUSE

Our Temple Marriage Stopped There

Married twenty years to an inactive husband, a Latter-day Saint wife talks about the frustrations and rewards.

By Jane Harveaux

Tom and I (not our real names) have been married for more than twenty years—married in the temple. But except for the months we dated before our marriage, Tom has been inactive. I knew in my heart that my sweetheart had not yet made a dedicated commitment to the Lord, but I felt sure that once we were married in the Lord's way, he would want nothing less than to live the gospel and honor his priesthood. However, no miracle took place within the temple's sacred walls. There have been times when despair and discouragement have weighed heavily on me, but we have stayed together through all the difficulty. And I am grateful.

From the first we could not kneel in prayer together. As the weeks rolled around, he found every excuse to be absent from meetings and priesthood duties. I found myself either staying home from church with him and feeling miserable, or going alone and feeling miserable. I felt hurt and betrayed. Why were the two things I loved the most in my life so incompatible? I loved Tom, yet I could not compromise my dedication to the gospel nor my desire to serve in the Church. I did not then realize—or care—what he must have been feeling too.

Raised in an inactive home, Tom did not actually sense the gospel as a dimension in his life. Furthermore, he had married a girl who said she loved the gospel and him but who never was happy! He was becoming miserable and uncommunicative because of what he saw as my selfish demands. For instance, Sunday was important to him as his own time—to sleep late, to fish, to golf, or go to the farm. But Sunday was important to me as the Lord's time—a holy day with sacred obligations. Time and again he would leave the house angry, and I would weep in bitter confusion. I felt estranged from Tom and the Lord. We were both beginning to feel regrets about our marriage.

One night, about a year and a half after we were married, I came to a crossroad quite unexpectedly. Pregnant with our first child, I didn't really feel like going to Primary preparation meeting that night. But I went. I shall never forget the impact of the inservice lesson. The objective was to help Primary workers know that if they live the gospel, the Lord will sustain them and guide their lives. The introduction read, "Because we are here to be tested and proved, the Lord does not make life easy for us. Every day we are passing or failing our tests depending on the decisions we make. If we choose the right regardless of the odds, He will see us through. Sybil's story illustrates this truth."

Sybil had my undivided attention at once. Both she and her husband Frank had been inactive for many years; the story began when their eldest child was ten and events had led her back to the Church. (I wondered if we would even be a family in ten years.) Frank's antagonism seemed to grow in direct proportion to Sybil's and the children's growth in the Church. While a longing to go to the temple was developing in Sybil, Frank withdrew, seeming more and more like a stranger. She expressed the same fright I felt—that their marriage was headed for dissolution. Should she try to save her marriage by becoming inactive again?

Her bishop's answer was my answer, too. I knew when I heard it that if I had the courage to change, there was still hope for Tom and me. He reminded us both that our husbands did not have the gospel in their lives and therefore could not understand our feelings. "'You must be more patient,' he counseled. 'Restore the good relation you used to have . . . by keeping in your mind all his goodness and letting him feel your love and appreciation and approval of him. Then let him know that . . . for you the Church meets an inner need. Try to have an understanding with him that if he will let you have the Church, you will let him live without it. In all other respects be the best wife you know how to be.'" (*Don't Close the Door*, Primary Inservice Lessons, 1959-60, pp. 140, 145-46). How these sentences resounded in my heart: In all other respects, be the best wife you know how to be. Let him feel your love and appreciation and approval. Restore the good relationship you used to have with him. You must be more patient!

Sybil's bishop concluded by reassuring, "The Lord wants you to stay with the Church and teach your children to love and obey Him. He will be with you." Then he gave her the Lord's promise, "Have not I commanded thee? Be strong and of a good courage; be not afraid, neither be thou dismayed: for the Lord thy God is with thee whithersoever thou goest." (Joshua 1:9.)

In Sybil's story, Frank returned to activity some six years later through two factors. First, Sybil had lived the counsel of her bishop—being a patient, loving wife. She taught the children to love and respect their father. Second, the Lord finally got Frank's attention through an accident that gave him sudden cause to reflect about what was really important. As I listened to Sybil's story, I took personal inventory. It was unpleasant to admit the need for so much repenting on my part; and though I could not imagine waiting six years for my "miracle," I began to live by that bishop's counsel. Almost at once our marriage improved.

But I am still waiting. Through the years I have often been discouraged in missing many blessings as a family. Tom did not have a desire to bless his sons as they were born, or baptize and confirm them, or confer the priesthood, or to bless us in illness. I was also discouraged because we were not having family home evening, or family prayer (except without Tom), or consistent blessings on the food, or gospel discussions with the children except in Tom's absence.

Tom is a good provider and has taught his sons the honor of honest labor as he works shoulder-to-shoulder with them on the farm. They love and respect their dad, but they have been hurt because he has not heard their talks or seen their programs or recitals or roadshows—or shared priesthood activities with them. When I have served as a teacher or counselor or president, I have never gotten used to Tom's lack of support, or to not being able to share spiritual matters heart-to-heart with him.

Consistent activity in the Church has been the source of rich blessings: My friendships and rapport with other women "alone" who do not waver in their testimonies have filled an important void in my life. And when I am where I ought to be, as I was the night I heard Sybil's story, I have always had access to the comfort and blessings of the priesthood. Such commitments always require extra planning, faith, and prayers, but I have learned these are the keys to receiving the Lord's help. The Relief Society has provided years of personal growth and help in raising my sons. Because I have remained close to the Lord, my children are close to him. Witnessing their growth in the Church and their love of the Lord, as they honor their parents and the priesthood, is my greatest joy. Our oldest son is serving a mission, and his brothers are making plans for theirs.

After years of no apparent change in Tom's attitude toward the Church, one day chapter 26 of Mosiah provided another essential clue for me. If a person does not believe in Christ and hardens his heart because of his lack of faith, he cannot understand the words of God. It finally became clear why Tom had rejected all our efforts, for only his own faith can provide him with insight and understanding. In other words, the Lord must first get Tom's attention.

The rest of the Lord's answer for me came when I learned my responsibility to fast and pray in Tom's behalf, as Alma prayed for his son in the Book of Mormon. (See Mosiah 27:14.) I realize that the Lord will probably not send an angel to get Tom's attention; instead he will use mortal servants with the same authority as the angel. Then it will be up to Tom to exercise his agency.

What if the "unthinkable" were to happen and Tom did not accept the gospel, even then? Again, Alma provides the answer. Once when he was weighed down with sorrow because he had not converted the people of a certain city, the same angel returned, comforting him: "Blessed art thou, Alma; therefore, lift up thy head and rejoice, for thou hast great cause to rejoice;

for thou hast been faithful in keeping the commandments of God from the time which thou receivedst thy first message from him." (Alma 8:15.)

We who have inactive and nonmember spouses have no cause to be weighed down with sorrow if we remain true and faithful. If we are downcast, always grieving for our mates, our lives can bless no one. If, on the other hand, we remain steadfast, cheerful, and optimistic, with the Lord's help we will have the capacity to work out our own salvation and radiate spiritual strength to those about us. Then when we meet our Savior we can gladly say that we have done our best.

I have been asked if I would make the same choice again. Twenty years ago, if I had known the difficult road ahead, I think I might have chosen another path. But the years have taught me patience; Sybil's formula has increased my love for Tom. I am now convinced the good man I married is worth waiting a lifetime for. My faith in his goodness still gives me hope. And my love of the gospel and my love for him are still the most precious things in my life.

Being Missionary to Your Spouse

"By gentleness and love unfeigned . . ."

By Mollie H. Sorensen

Unspeakable joy came over me as my husband walked to the stand to be sustained second counselor in the stake presidency. As he bore his testimony of his love for the Savior and of the gospel, he also gave thanks for his wife. I recalled the time I came home and found a poster tacked up on the dining room wall, proclaiming, "I love my wife because she has faith in me!"

It seemed not long ago that he emphatically announced, "They'd better not ever ask me to give a sacrament meeting talk, because that's something I'll never do." He now is one of the favorite speakers in the stake. I remembered, too, that my husband had said: "Just because you're into dramatics, don't think you can persuade me to be in a play. I'm just not an actor." He was great in the lead part of a stake play. "I'm not a reader," he had insisted. Now he reads the scriptures faithfully every day and teaches them to all of us each morning. "I don't understand how to use the priesthood," he once said. But since then he has blessed our family with the power of the priesthood on numerous occasions. Yes, my husband has changed! Sixteen years ago he was a prospective elder.

What has brought about this mighty change? For my sisters who stand in the perplexing situation of being missionary to their husbands, I would like to share a few insights. Since I speak from experience, I speak as a wife. But the principles could be used as well by a husband who has need of being missionary to his wife.

It is not easy to have faith in your spouse if he has disappointed you over and over. And for the woman who enjoys spiritual truths, it is frustrating not to be able to openly share them. Her desire to have her husband understand and appreciate the gospel becomes almost unbearable at times. And this is normal; for having achieved great joy, the natural consequence is to want to share it with loved ones.

But in these cases, a very delicate situation can arise. The man is the head of the house—the one who should lead, not be led. The woman, while being an equal partner in the marriage, should support and sustain her husband in taking his leadership role. But if he is not active or isn't a member of the Church, she is placed in a very frustrating position. Often, if she wants Sabbath attendance, family home evenings, and other Church activities, she faces an inner battle and may even have open conflict with her husband—thus defeating her purpose to bring unity and spirituality into the home.

Where can a woman go for guidance and direction in her role as missionary to her husband? Great insights can be found through studying the scriptures. For example, I learned an important lesson when I studied about the council in heaven and the issues discussed there. Satan proposed a plan of forcing everyone to obey the principles of their Father in Heaven. "I will redeem all mankind," he said, "that one soul shall not be lost, and surely I will do it." But Heavenly Father did not want "to destroy the agency of man, which I, the Lord God, had given him." Instead, he made available the plan of salvation through his Only Begotten Son, whereby we could enjoy freedom of choice. (See Moses 4:1-4.)

From this scriptural account, we can conclude that trying to force another to accept the gospel is not pleasing to our Father. He cares not only that they return again to him, but also that they do so of their own free will and choice. He wants them to discover for themselves that the truths he has given are right and good and will bring the greatest joy. In order to do this, everyone needs to be free to experience and discover for himself.

Some true methods of exerting influence are listed in the Doctrine and Covenants: "Only by persuasion, by long-suffering, by gentleness and meekness, and by love unfeigned. By kindness, and pure knowledge, which shall greatly enlarge the soul without hypocrisy, and without guile." (D&C 121:41-42.) These qualities, the Lord's methods of persuasion, can become part of our very nature if we live worthy to obtain an endowment of his Spirit. I've learned that although a wife can encourage and be a light unto her husband, it is still the Spirit of the Lord that changes lives.

In Galatians 5:22-23 we find: "The fruit of the Spirit is love, joy, peace, longsuffering, gentleness, goodness, faith, meekness, temperance." There are those who would counsel wives to *pretend* to have these qualities of love, gentleness, and meekness in order to establish a better relationship with their husbands. But in this pretense or guile, they bypass the Savior, who condemned hypocrisy.

I have found that the very core of our being must be purged of its natural inclination to criticize and to lose faith. To do this, we must obtain greater power than we alone possess. Heavenly Father can give us this ability to change—to make a faultfinding, sour disposition sweet again, as a little child's. "Create in me a clean heart, O God," we might plead; "and renew a right spirit within me." (Psalm 51:10.) He can bless us with the ability to see better, to uncover beautiful and lovable qualities of character in our spouses.

Although it may not be easy to love those who have disappointed us, we are promised that the Spirit can endow us with the power to love even those whose actions make them difficult to love: "Wherefore, my beloved brethren, pray unto the Father with all the energy of heart, that ye may be filled with this love, which he hath bestowed upon all who are true followers of his Son, Jesus Christ." (Moroni 7:48.)

One woman who attained this loving nature with the Spirit's help expressed it in this way: "There was a time when I was so frustrated with what my husband *wasn't* doing that I didn't appreciate the good he *was* doing. I was hung up on the letter of the law and forgot the more important things, such as love, patience, forgiveness, and faith. I seemed obsessed with impatience for him to change. Then somehow, I realized I was wrong. I knew my attitude towards my husband was without hope. I sought Heavenly Father for a change of heart, praying and fasting. Like a miracle, gradually my heart began to change. The more I felt the warmth of the Spirit in my life, the more I lost the compulsion to criticize. Not only that, but I was able to love and respect him in ways that I had overlooked before. I began deeply appreciating his patience with the children, his tolerance for others, his cheerful disposition, and his way of working with his hands—he could accomplish in one hour what many men would in half a day! Oh, of course I still wish he would become active in the Church, but I've gained a real tolerance for him to grow in his own way, and I pray that I will be the example of love that he needs in order to feel free to grow. I want him to see by my actions that the gospel of Jesus Christ is really wonderful, sweet, and exciting."

Contrast this with the woman who uses bitterness, anger, hopelessness, and the spirit of contention as her tools of persuasion. In her frustration to have things right, she displays an example of what the gospel of Jesus Christ is *not*—pushing her husband further away and leaving him without a taste of its goodness. Satan would thwart us in our attempts to influence with love, for it is truly our most powerful tool. He would have us be contentious and exercise coercion. He would have us neglect our own spiritual nourishment—prayer, fasting, study—for a fury of impatience. He would have us be as the Pharisees, nit-picking over practices and forgetting principles.

It is right, for example, to have family home evenings. But it is not right for a wife to force her husband, through embarrassment, into this practice. There are times when wives of inactive or nonmember husbands must be content to leave part of the law undone and patiently wait for their husbands to lead the way. In such cases, the "weightier matters of the law" (Matthew 23:23) need not be left undone—for these are the gifts of the Spirit, which will help a wife "have no more disposition to do evil [nag, preach, judge], but to do good continually" to her husband (see Mosiah 5:2).

We have all probably experienced being caught up in the

spirit of a meeting and enjoying the feelings of warmth and love. As we drive home, the feeling lingers. The whole world looks different—filled with love, excitement, and promise. The same children whose prattlings may have disturbed us on the way to the meeting now seem to glow with angelic countenance. Such is the influence of the Spirit, which is love, peace, and joy. We should plead for this influence daily. Only with it are we able to overcome and block Satan's efforts to destroy our marriages.

One woman came up to me in tears after Relief Society one day and said, "I'm about ready to give up on him. I thought a year would bring some changes, but he's no more ready to become active than he was last year. I feel like the Lord has failed me. Why should I keep trying if he'll never change?"

After listening and searching for understanding, I asked, "You say you are still trying. Have you been devoting yourself to your own spiritual nourishment lately, as you were a year ago when you felt such promise for the relationship?"

"No," she answered, "I haven't felt like praying and with moving to another home, I haven't felt like I've had time for studying."

"Well," I confided, "I know that when I begin to lose faith in my husband and in our relationship, or when I start to become critical, I find that I have been starving my own spirit. But as I begin to restore a sweet spirit within me, I see my husband with new faith and love."

A few weeks later, this woman called to tell me that through recommitting herself to a program of spiritual feedings, she once again had hope in her husband and in their marriage. She said, "I was wrong. There has been a change in him. It is so slight that I had overlooked it before."

Each week when we partake of the bread and water in remembrance of the Savior, we are given the promise that if we keep his commandments, we will have his Spirit to be with us. And with his Spirit, spouses may know how best to truly be a help and a strength to each other.

Mollie H. Sorensen, mother of ten and a 1981 graduate of Brigham Young University, teaches Sunday School in her Napa, California, ward.

Changing Me Changed Our Marriage

We can greatly improve our marriages by taking stock of ourselves . . .

I'm married to a non-Mormon. Though I sincerely want my husband to join the Church, I've found that I need not wait until then to have a marriage that is a bit of heaven on earth. I'm happy at home, and so is my husband. But it certainly didn't start that way.

For the first seven years Brent and I were married, I nagged. Not a lot, mind you, but my husband certainly knew that he smoked too much, went out with the boys too often, didn't spend enough time with me and the children, didn't handle money very well, drank too much, and didn't do enough chores around the house.

I had two things going for me though. An earlier divorce had made me vow that I would never leave Brent and that he would never leave without knowing I loved him and wanted him to stay. Consequently, although he packed his bags a couple of times, he never walked out with them.

The other point was that we both had loving natures and a deep regard for each other. Sometimes it got hidden by the anger, but it was always there. Still, his life-style created frustrations for me. I realized that Brent wasn't changing, and my frustrations were making home life unpleasant. One day in Relief Society we were told that the woman sets the tone of the home. That made me think, and I began looking for articles and books to help me. I sat down with myself and analyzed what I was doing.

The first thing I saw was that seven years of nagging had produced no results; Brent knew by now what I didn't like, so I might as well stop repeating myself. Second, if I couldn't change him I would have to change *me* and find ways to live cheerfully with what he was. I needed to work on my perfection, not his. Third, I could never love him as I should if I was constantly thinking I might someday have to choose between him and the Church. Fourth, I must let him take his rightful place as head of the family in all things, even decisions involving the Church.

From Relief Society lessons, Sunday School classes, personal scripture study, BYU Education Weeks, various books, and much prayer, I developed a plan. I decided to begin by remaining cheerful when Brent stayed out late. Prayer was the key to this change. The first time Brent came home late to find me in a good mood, his reaction was, "What's going on here?" I told him I was wasting too much energy worrying about him and so was asking our Heavenly Father to take care of him because he had more influence on circumstances than I had. I also said that Brent had enough sense to keep himself out of trouble. He laughed, and within two months was phoning me if he planned on being late. He was also coming home consistently earlier since he had a pleasant wife to come home to. It was hard. I had to discipline myself; when I couldn't contain myself after he arrived home from drinking late, I learned to leave the house. But the results were worth it; our quarrels over Brent's drinking were drastically reduced.

Buoyed by that good experience, I sought new ways to eliminate other points of contention. I quit nagging Brent to take us places. Instead, I planned outings and family home evenings for us, then invited him to come with us. Sometimes he did; sometimes he didn't. We were glad to have him with us, but went ahead without him if he was busy. I also invited myself along if he was going somewhere we would enjoy. If he said no, I didn't let it bother me. Even more important, I began finding ways to communicate my love. I began thanking him for every chore done and every compliment, gift, good turn, considerate action, and show of affection he gave me. I also started complimenting him on the way he dressed, on his sense of humor—on every good point I noticed. Needless to say, I began seeing more and more good things about him. The more I saw, the more my respect grew, and the more I loved him.

Slowly I learned to really think of him as the head of the house. I learned to go to him and ask for his help when I had a problem instead of accusing and blaming whenever I made a mistake. Doors of communication that had been shut for years began opening. Then, carefully, I started asking his permission to go to church functions or take the children somewhere. At first he said, "Go ahead. You'll do it anyway." But by not doing things I knew he objected to, he eventually learned I honored his wishes and he took more interest in what we were doing.

And I worked on me. Brent disliked to come home to unwashed dishes, so I resolved to have the dishes done no matter what else was left. I also resolved to get more sleep so I'd be more pleasant to come home to. I studied, planned my schedule, and then replanned it. My children helped more willingly after I told them I needed their help in making our home a happy place. I lost some weight, dressed more neatly, and let my hair grow a little longer because Brent likes it better that way. I especially worked on forgetting what I wanted Brent to do for me and concentrated on what I could do to make him feel more loved.

It is now four years later and I am still working on all of these areas, but the blessings can't be counted. Months ago Brent paid me the supreme compliment of saying he would never have had the confidence to recently start his own business without my support. Daily I feel loved and cherished. A smile over the heads of our children, holding my hand as we walk down the street, his teasing to make me laugh, telephone calls to let me know he misses me, small gifts that say "I love you," a lunch date without the children—all these things show me he loves me. And when he tells me he wants us to be married forever, I am completely happy.

He has changed greatly. He has quit smoking, cut his drinking down, enjoys spending time with us, and takes one child at a time on a special outing every few weeks. He is a kind, loving husband and father, interested in what we do and think and feel.

Our love for him is possibly helping him move toward baptism. But if he chooses not to join the Church, the love and peace in our home, and the growth and development I've experienced through trying to apply gospel principles is reward enough.

Bibliography

Note: All articles originated in the *Ensign*.

Baker, Terry R. "When Marriages Have Problems." February 1980, pp. 6-8.

Barlow, Brent A. "Getting to Know You Better." September 1981, pp. 43-45.

Burton, Rulon T. "The Dangers of Debt in Marriage." September 1984, pp. 49-52.

Card, Orson Scott. "Family Finances." June 1978, pp. 12-17.

"Changing Me, Changed Our Marriage." January 1981, pp. 8-9.

Chidester, C. Richard. "A Change of Heart: Key to Harmonious Relationships." February 1984, pp. 6-11.

Chidester, C. Richard. "Keeping in Touch with Feelings." July 1979, pp. 15-17.

Clement, C. Ross. "Breaking the Cycle." September 1981, pp. 38-41.

Cole, Carole Osborne. "After the Temple." April 1978, pp. 49-51.

Coombs, David H. "Developing Sensitivity in Marriage." October 1979, pp. 39-41.

Dahl, Paul E. "Keeping Your Marriage Alive." July 1982, pp. 56-60.

Day, Afton J. "To Change Your Marriage, Change Yourself." August 1976, pp. 38-41.

Ellsworth, Dr. Homer. "Sacred Power, Used With Wisdom." August 1979, pp. 23-24.

England, Kathy. "Love That Lasts." February 1982, pp. 47-49.

Gardner, Marvin K. "Really, Is It Any Wonder I Love Her?" December 1980, pp. 17-21.

Gilliland, Steve. "Chastity: A Principle of Power." June 1980, pp. 16-19.

Gilliland, Steve. "Winning the Argument or Solving the Problem." October 1980, pp. 20-24.

Hafen, Bruce C. "Individual Liberty, Commitment, and Marriage." December 1978, pp. 14-17.

Hansen, Jennie L. "The Best Gift." July 1982, p. 39.

Harper, James M. "Let's Help This Marriage Grow." August 1983, pp. 25-27.

Harveaux, Jane. "Our Temple Marriage Stopped There." August 1978, pp. 27-29.

"Keeping the Marriage Covenant Sacred." August 1981, pp. 22-24.

Long, Judith. "The Formula That Saved Our Marriage." March 1983, pp. 14-17.

Olson, Terrance D. "The Compassionate Marriage Partner." August 1982, pp. 14-17.

Sorenson, Mollie H. "Being Missionary to Your Spouse." September 1983, pp. 58-61.

Index

Index